Christmas
with Southern Living
Cookbook
Volume 3

Christmas
with Southern Living
Cookbook

Volume 3

*Enrich your holiday celebrations with this
all-new collection of menus, recipes, and
food gift ideas.*

Oxmoor
House®

©1999 by Oxmoor House, Inc.
Book Division of Southern Progress Corporation
P.O. Box 2463, Birmingham, Alabama 35201

Southern Living® is a federally registered trademark belonging to
    Southern Living, Inc.

ISBN: 0-8487-1895-X
ISSN: 1099-4386

Printed in the United States of America
Fourth Printing 2001

Editor-in-Chief: Nancy Fitzpatrick Wyatt
Senior Foods Editor: Susan Carlisle Payne
Senior Editor, Copy and Homes: Olivia Kindig Wells
Art Director: James Boone

Christmas with Southern Living® Cookbook Volume 3
Editor: Kelly Hooper Troiano
Copy Editor: Donna Baldone
Editorial Assistant: Allison Long
Director, Test Kitchens: Kathleen Royal Phillips
Assistant Director, Test Kitchens: Gayle Hays Sadler
Test Kitchens Staff: Julie Christopher, Natalie E. King,
    Rebecca Mohr, Jan A. Smith, Kate M. Wheeler, R.D.
Senior Photographer: Jim Bathie
Photographer: Brit Huckabay
Senior Photo Stylist: Kay E. Clarke
Photo Stylists: Virginia R. Cravens, Lydia E. DeGaris, Jan Gautro
Director, Production and Distribution: Phillip Lee
Associate Production Manager: Theresa L. Beste
Production Assistant: Faye Porter Bonner

CONTRIBUTORS:
Designer: Rita Yerby
Copy Editor: Shari K. Wimberley
Indexer: Mary Ann Laurens
Photo Stylist: Melanie J. Clarke
Test Kitchens Staff: Lorrie Hulston, L. Victoria Knowles

Cover: White Chocolate Poinsettia Cake (page 118)
Back Cover: Praline Chicken, Rosemary Roasted Potatoes, and
    Steamed Green Beans (page 67)
Page 2: Pork with Red Plum Sauce (page 89) and Wild Mushroom
    and Onion Risotto (page 96), and Steamed Broccoli

(page 17)

We Want Your Favorite Recipes!

Southern Living cooks are simply the best cooks, and we
want your secrets! Please send your favorite original
recipes and a sentence about why you like each one. We
can't guarantee we'll print them in a cookbook, but if we
do, we'll send you $20 and a free copy of the cookbook.
Send each recipe on a separate page, with your name,
address, and daytime phone number to:

Cookbook Recipes
Oxmoor House
2100 Lakeshore Drive
Birmingham, AL 35209

(page 107)

(page 99)

(page 78)

Contents

Menu on page 11.

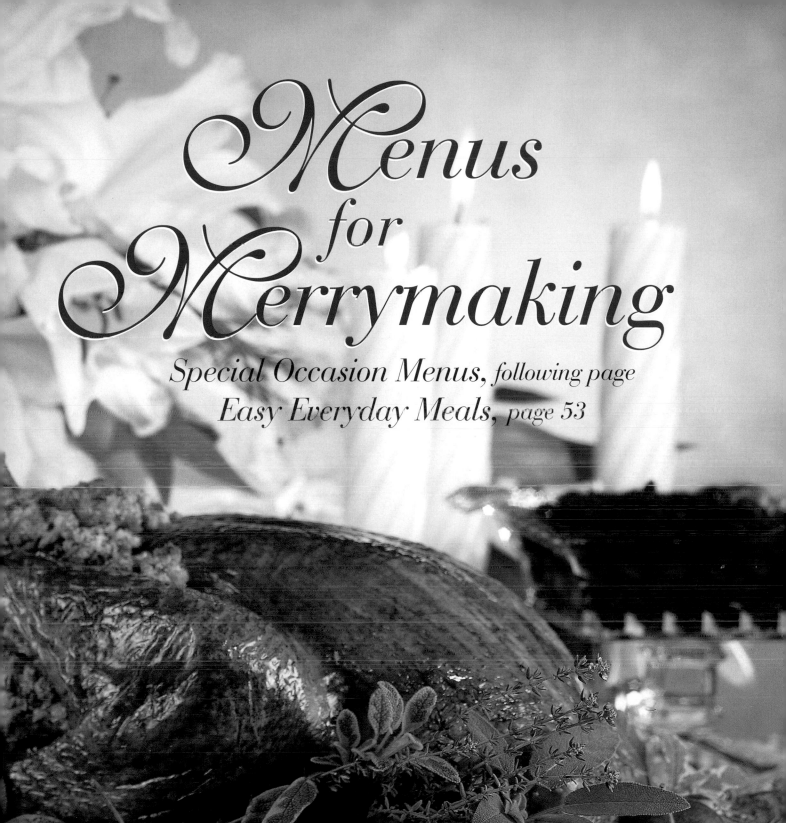

Menus for Merrymaking

Special Occasion Menus, following page
Easy Everyday Meals, page 53

Special Occasion Menus

This is the season for sharing. And what better way than by extending warm Southern hospitality to the special people in your life. Whether you want a large feast or an intimate gathering, we have 10 delectable menus to fit any festive occasion. Flip through these pages to find scrumptious recipes, make-ahead suggestions, tips, plus handy shopping lists to ease your efforts in providing good food and lasting memories.

Big Feast Menu
(following page)

Big Feast

MINNESOTA WILD RICE SOUP

TURKEY WITH OYSTER STUFFING

GREEN BEANS SUPREME

BUTTERED CARROTS

WHOLE-BERRY CRANBERRY SAUCE

CHRISTMAS AMBROSIA

BAKERY ROLLS OR
EASY BUTTERY CRESCENT ROLLS (PAGE 110)

CHOCOLATE-CARAMEL PECAN PIE

Serves 10 to 12

Gather family and friends for a traditional feast this Christmas. They'll come back for seconds of favorites such as Turkey with Oyster Stuffing, cheesy green beans, and ambrosia. Our shopping list includes bakery rolls; if you prefer to make your own, add those ingredients to the list. A chocolate-inspired variation of pecan pie ends this glorious feast—make two pies to serve 10 to 12 people.

SHOPPING LIST

Staples: all-purpose flour, butter or margarine, milk, salt, pepper, powdered sugar, sugar, vanilla extract
. . . .

Herbs and Spices: bay leaves, dried chervil, ground cloves, whole cloves, curry powder, ground mace, dry mustard, rubbed sage, dried thyme
. . . .

1 bunch fresh parsley
3 pounds carrots
1 bunch celery
1 (8-ounce) package sliced fresh mushrooms
6 large onions
1 green pepper
1 coconut (or 3 cups grated)
18 small oranges
. . . .

8 ounces process American cheese, shredded
1 pint half-and-half
1 (16-ounce) carton sour cream
½ pint whipping cream
3 (16-ounce) bags frozen cut green beans
. . . .

Bakery rolls
1 cup fine, dry breadcrumbs
Bread for 12 cups soft breadcrumbs
6 slices bacon
2 (12-ounce) containers Standard oysters
1 (10- to 12-pound) turkey
2 quarts chicken broth
1 (16-ounce) can whole-berry cranberry sauce
2 (14-ounce) packages caramels
2 (8-ounce) packages semisweet chocolate squares
2 (15¼-ounce) cans crushed pineapple
⅔ cup dry sherry
6 cups chopped pecans
1 cup chopped walnuts
1 (6-ounce) package wild rice
. . . .

Garnishes: maraschino cherries with stems, fresh chives, sage, thyme, crabapples, kumquats

MINNESOTA WILD RICE SOUP

Chervil, a mild-flavored member of the parsley family, adds distinctive flavor to this special-occasion soup.

1 (6-ounce) package wild rice
1 cup finely chopped onion
1 teaspoon salt
1 teaspoon dried chervil
1 teaspoon curry powder
½ teaspoon dry mustard
½ teaspoon pepper
¼ cup butter or margarine, melted

1 (8-ounce) package sliced fresh mushrooms
½ cup thinly sliced celery
½ cup all-purpose flour
6 cups chicken broth
2 cups half-and-half
⅔ cup dry sherry
Garnish: fresh chives

Cook wild rice according to package directions.

Meanwhile, cook onion and next 5 ingredients in butter in a large Dutch oven over medium-high heat, stirring constantly, until onion is tender. Add mushrooms and celery; cook, stirring constantly, until mushrooms are tender. Reduce heat to low. Add flour, stirring until blended. Cook 1 minute, stirring constantly. Gradually add chicken broth; cook over medium heat, stirring constantly, until slightly thickened. Stir in cooked rice, half-and-half, and sherry; cook until thoroughly heated. To serve, ladle soup into individual soup bowls. Garnish, if desired. Yield: 12 cups.

TURKEY WITH OYSTER STUFFING

You'll hear lots of oohs and aahs once guests sample this fragrant herb- and oyster-laced stuffing.

4 large onions, chopped (about 4½ cups) and divided
2 medium carrots, scraped and chopped (about 1 cup)
1 stalk celery, chopped (about ½ cup)
12 sprigs fresh parsley
3 sprigs fresh celery leaves
2 sprigs fresh thyme or ½ teaspoon dried thyme
2 bay leaves
2 whole cloves, crushed
1 (10- to 12-pound) turkey
1½ cups finely chopped fresh celery leaves
2 tablespoons chopped green pepper
2 tablespoons chopped fresh parsley

1 teaspoon rubbed sage
½ teaspoon salt
½ teaspoon pepper
½ teaspoon dried thyme
½ teaspoon ground mace
½ teaspoon ground cloves
1 cup butter or margarine, melted
12 cups soft breadcrumbs (homemade)
2 (12-ounce) containers Standard oysters, drained and chopped
6 slices bacon
1 to 2 cups chicken broth
3 tablespoons all-purpose flour
Garnishes: fresh sage, fresh thyme, crabapples, kumquats

Place 1½ cups chopped onion, carrot, and next 6 ingredients in bottom of a large roasting pan; set aside.

Remove giblets and neck from turkey; reserve for another use. Rinse turkey thoroughly with cold water; pat dry. Place turkey, breast side up, on a rack in prepared pan. Set aside.

Cook remaining chopped onion, chopped celery leaves, and next 8 ingredients in butter in a large skillet over medium-high heat, stirring constantly, until tender. Combine onion mixture, breadcrumbs, and oysters in a large bowl. Set aside.

Cook bacon in a large skillet until crisp; remove bacon, reserving ¼ cup drippings. Reserve bacon for another use.

Spoon 2 cups oyster mixture into body cavity of turkey. Spoon remaining oyster mixture into a lightly greased 11- x 7- x 1½-inch baking dish, and refrigerate. Tie ends of legs together with string. Lift wingtips up and over back, and tuck under bird. Rub entire surface of turkey with bacon drippings.

Cover pan with heavy-duty aluminum foil, being careful not to let foil touch turkey. Bake at 325° for 3 to 3½ hours. Uncover and bake 1 additional hour or until a meat thermometer inserted in meaty portion of thigh registers 180° and stuffing registers 165°.

Bake oyster mixture in baking dish at 325°, uncovered, for 45 minutes or until golden.

Transfer turkey to a large serving platter, reserving drippings in pan. Pour drippings through a wire-mesh strainer into a liquid measuring cup, discarding solids. Skim fat from drippings. Add enough chicken broth to drippings to measure 2 cups.

Combine 2 cups drippings and flour in a medium saucepan, stirring with a wire whisk until mixture is smooth. Cook over medium heat, stirring constantly, until mixture thickens slightly. Serve gravy with turkey. Garnish, if desired. Yield: 10 to 12 servings.

Remember that end-point temperatures are critical when cooking stuffed poultry. Always stuff the bird just before you put it in the oven, never ahead. Bake until stuffing temperature reaches 165°. Immediately remove and refrigerate any stufffing leftover from turkey cavity. Reheat thoroughly until hot and steaming (165°).

GREEN BEANS SUPREME

3 (16-ounce) bags frozen cut green
   beans
1 cup sliced onion
2 tablespoons minced fresh parsley
¼ cup butter or margarine, melted
   and divided
¼ cup all-purpose flour

2 teaspoons salt
½ teaspoon pepper
1 (16-ounce) carton sour cream
2 cups (8 ounces) shredded process
   American cheese
1 cup fine, dry breadcrumbs
   (store-bought)

Cook green beans according to package directions; drain well, and set aside.

Cook onion and parsley in 2 tablespoons butter in a large skillet over medium-high heat, stirring constantly, until tender. Reduce heat to medium-low. Stir in flour, salt, and pepper. Add sour cream, stirring well. Add green beans; cook until thoroughly heated, stirring occasionally.

Spoon mixture into an ungreased 13- x 9- x 2-inch baking dish; sprinkle with cheese. Combine breadcrumbs and remaining 2 tablespoons butter; sprinkle over cheese. Bake at 350° for 20 minutes or until cheese melts and breadcrumbs are browned. Yield: 12 servings.

CHRISTMAS AMBROSIA

Oranges, pineapple, and coconut make a versatile fruit dish to serve as a side dish or light dessert.

18 small oranges
2 (15¼-ounce) cans crushed
   pineapple, undrained
3 cups grated fresh, canned, or
   frozen coconut

1 cup chopped walnuts, toasted
Whipped cream (optional)
Garnish: maraschino cherries with
   stems

Peel and section oranges, catching juice in a large nonmetal bowl. Add orange sections, pineapple, and coconut to juice; toss gently. Cover and chill thoroughly.

To serve, stir in toasted walnuts, and spoon fruit mixture into individual dishes; top each serving with a dollop of whipped cream. Garnish, if desired. Yield: 10 to 12 servings.

CHOCOLATE-CARAMEL PECAN PIE

2 cups finely chopped pecans
¼ cup sugar
¼ cup butter or margarine, melted
1 (14-ounce) package caramels
¼ cup milk
1 cup chopped pecans

8 (1-ounce) squares semisweet
   chocolate
⅓ cup milk
¼ cup sifted powdered sugar
½ teaspoon vanilla extract

For this menu, prepare two pies to serve 12; do not double recipe.

Combine first 3 ingredients in a small bowl; stir well. Firmly press mixture in bottom and up sides of a 9-inch pieplate. Bake at 350° for 12 minutes. Cool completely on a wire rack.

Unwrap caramels, and place in a medium saucepan. Add ¼ cup milk; cook over low heat until caramels melt, stirring often. Remove from heat, and pour over prepared crust. Sprinkle 1 cup chopped pecans over caramel mixture.

Combine chocolate, ⅓ cup milk, powdered sugar, and vanilla in a heavy saucepan. Cook over low heat until chocolate melts, stirring constantly. Drizzle melted chocolate mixture evenly over pecans. Cover and chill at least 2 hours. Yield: one 9-inch pie.

A Simple Celebration

HERBED LEG OF LAMB

HEARTS OF PALM SALAD

SQUASH ROLLS

COMPANY COCONUT CAKE

Serves 6

Streamline your holiday celebration with four simple but sensational recipes. Guests will rave over the leg of lamb that is stuffed with a savory herb mixture and topped with breadcrumbs. Serve Hearts of Palm Salad as an easy side, and offer hot tender rolls that are sure to please and surprise your guests—they're made with yellow squash. Top the evening off with Company Coconut Cake, and your celebration is a success.

SHOPPING LIST

Staples: all-purpose flour, butter or margarine, Dijon mustard, milk, olive oil, vegetable oil, salt, pepper, shortening, sugar, vanilla extract, white wine vinegar

. . . .

Herbs and Spices: dried basil, ground mace, ground nutmeg, dried rosemary, dried tarragon, dried thyme

. . . .

2 teaspoons chopped fresh chives
3 cloves garlic
6 cups mixed baby salad greens
3 tablespoons chopped fresh parsley
3 large yellow squash
1 large tomato

. . . .

3 large eggs
1 (8-ounce) package cream cheese
1 (8-ounce) carton sour cream

. . . .

6 slices white bread
1 (14.4-ounce) can hearts of palm
1 (6½-pound) boneless leg of lamb, butterflied
¼ cup shelled pistachio nuts
1 (¼-ounce) envelope active dry yeast
¾ cup cream of coconut
1 (7-ounce) can flaked coconut
1 (18.25-ounce) package white cake mix with pudding
1 (16-ounce) package powdered sugar

. . . .

Garnish: fresh rosemary sprigs

HERBED LEG OF LAMB

6 slices white bread, crusts removed
2 cloves garlic
3 tablespoons chopped fresh parsley
2 teaspoons chopped fresh chives
1 teaspoon dried thyme
1 teaspoon dried rosemary
½ teaspoon salt
⅛ teaspoon pepper
¼ cup shelled pistachio nuts
1 (6½-pound) boneless leg of lamb, butterflied
Garnish: fresh rosemary sprigs

Position knife blade in food processor bowl; add 4 bread slices. Process 20 seconds or until bread is crumbly. Remove breadcrumbs from food processor; set aside.

Drop garlic through food chute with processor running; process 5 seconds. Add remaining 2 bread slices, parsley, and next 6 ingredients; process 15 seconds.

Trim excess fat from lamb. Spread herb mixture over inner surface of lamb. Roll roast, starting at shortest end; tie securely with heavy string at 2-inch intervals.

Coat entire surface of lamb with reserved breadcrumbs, patting to secure crumbs.

Place lamb, seam side down, on a rack in a roasting pan. Bake at 425° for 30 minutes. Reduce heat to 350°; bake 2½ hours or until a meat thermometer inserted in thickest part registers 150° (medium-rare). Remove from oven. Cover with aluminum foil; let stand 20 minutes before serving. Garnish, if desired. Yield: 10 servings.

HEARTS OF PALM SALAD

1 clove garlic, minced
⅓ cup olive oil
2 tablespoons white wine vinegar
1 tablespoon Dijon mustard
½ teaspoon salt
½ teaspoon pepper
⅛ teaspoon dried tarragon
⅛ teaspoon dried basil
⅛ teaspoon dried thyme
6 cups mixed baby salad greens
1 (14.4-ounce) can hearts of palm, drained and cut into bite-size pieces
1 large tomato, cut into wedges

Combine first 9 ingredients in a bowl; stir until blended. Cover; chill 4 hours.

Combine salad greens, hearts of palm, and tomato in a large bowl. Pour dressing over salad; toss gently. Serve salad immediately. Yield: 6 servings.

SQUASH ROLLS

Pureed squash tenderizes these dinner rolls. Your family will love them.

1¾ cups chopped yellow squash
1 cup water
1 (¼-ounce) envelope active dry yeast
½ cup warm water (105° to 115°)
½ cup warm milk (105° to 115°)
3 cups all-purpose flour, divided
¼ cup sugar
¼ cup shortening
1 teaspoon salt
½ teaspoon ground nutmeg
¼ teaspoon ground mace

Combine squash and 1 cup water in a saucepan; bring to a boil. Reduce heat; simmer, uncovered, 20 minutes or until squash is very tender. Drain well.

Position knife blade in food processor bowl; add squash. Process until smooth, stopping once to scrape down sides. Set aside.

Combine yeast and ½ cup water in a 1-cup liquid measuring cup; let stand 5 minutes.

Combine squash, yeast mixture, milk, 2 cups flour, sugar, and remaining 4 ingredients in a large mixing bowl; beat at medium speed of an electric mixer until well blended. Gradually stir in enough remaining 1 cup flour to make a soft dough. (Dough will be sticky.)

Turn dough out onto a well-floured surface, and knead until smooth and elastic (about 5 minutes). Place in a well-greased bowl, turning to grease top.

Cover and let rise in a warm place (85°), free from drafts, 1 hour or until doubled in bulk.

Punch dough down; divide into 18 portions. (Dough will be sticky.) Shape each portion into a ball; place 2 inches apart on lightly greased baking sheets.

Cover and let rise in a warm place, free from drafts, 40 minutes or until doubled in bulk. Bake at 400° for 12 to 15 minutes or until golden. Yield: 1½ dozen.

COMPANY COCONUT CAKE

3 large eggs
1 (8-ounce) carton sour cream
¾ cup vegetable oil
¾ cup cream of coconut
½ teaspoon vanilla extract
1 (18.25-ounce) package white cake mix with pudding
Coconut-Cream Cheese Frosting

Grease and flour three 8-inch round cakepans. Set pans aside.

Beat eggs at high speed of an electric mixer 2 minutes. Add sour cream and next 3 ingredients, beating well after each addition. Add cake mix; beat at low speed until blended. Beat at high speed 2 minutes. Pour batter into prepared pans.

Bake at 325° for 35 minutes or until a wooden pick inserted in center comes out clean. Cool in pans on wire racks 10 minutes. Remove from pans; cool completely on wire racks. Spread Coconut-Cream Cheese Frosting between layers and on top and sides of cake. Store in refrigerator in an airtight container. Yield: one 3-layer cake.

COCONUT-CREAM CHEESE FROSTING

1 (8-ounce) package cream cheese, softened
½ cup butter or margarine, softened
1 teaspoon vanilla extract
1 (16-ounce) package powdered sugar, sifted
1 (7-ounce) can flaked coconut

Beat cream cheese and butter at medium speed of an electric mixer until creamy. Add vanilla, beating well. Gradually add sugar, beating until smooth. Stir in coconut. Yield: 4 cups.

If you avoid baking coconut cake because you think it's too involved, then you're in for a pleasant surprise. This version features convenient cake mix as the main ingredient, but tastes just like it's made from scratch. We gave it our highest rating.

Christmas Eve Dinner

Elegant Pimiento Soup

Royal Beef Tenderloin

Potato Puff Soufflé

Winter Salad with Raspberry Vinaigrette

Bakery Rolls

Triple Chocolate Ecstasy (page 117)

Serves 6

Holiday spirits will sparkle as guests are treated to this special Christmas Eve celebration. The pastel colored pimiento soup serves as a fine first course followed by savory beef tenderloin—and don't pass up the Royal Butter that accompanies the beef. You'll also enjoy Raspberry Vinaigrette over a fresh fruit salad, and feast on Triple Chocolate Ecstasy for the grand finale.

ELEGANT PIMIENTO SOUP

5 cups chicken broth, divided
2 (7-ounce) jars diced pimientos,
   drained
¼ cup plus 1 tablespoon butter or
   margarine

¼ cup all-purpose flour
3 cups half-and-half
Salt and freshly ground pepper to
   taste
Garnishes: sour cream, fresh dill

Combine 2 cups chicken broth and pimiento in a saucepan; bring to a boil. Remove from heat; cool slightly. Pour pimiento mixture into container of an electric blender; cover and process until smooth, stopping once to scrape down sides.

Melt butter in a saucepan over low heat. Add flour, stirring until smooth. Cook 1 minute, stirring constantly. Gradually add half-and-half; cook over medium heat, stirring constantly, until mixture is thickened and bubbly. Reduce heat to low; add remaining 3 cups broth, pimiento mixture, and salt and pepper to taste. Cook until heated, stirring occasionally. To serve, ladle into individual soup bowls. Serve immediately, or cover and chill. Garnish, if desired. Yield: 9 cups.

ROYAL BEEF TENDERLOIN

The perfect entrée for a special occasion or Sunday dinner, this tenderloin and flavored butter can also be served as an appetizer on small dinner rolls.

1 cup soy sauce
⅔ cup vegetable oil
3 tablespoons brown sugar
2 tablespoons Dijon mustard
1 tablespoon white vinegar
1 teaspoon garlic powder

1 green onion, chopped
1 (5- to 6-pound) beef tenderloin,
   trimmed
Garnishes: fresh crimini and shiitake
   mushrooms, flat-leaf parsley
Royal Butter

Combine first 7 ingredients; stir well. Place tenderloin in a large heavy-duty, zip-top plastic bag. Pour marinade mixture over tenderloin. Seal bag securely. Marinate in refrigerator 8 hours, turning occasionally. Remove tenderloin from marinade, reserving marinade. Bring marinade to a boil in a small saucepan; set aside.

Place tenderloin on a rack in a shallow roasting pan. Bake at 400° for 45 to 55 minutes or until thermometer inserted in thickest part registers 145° (medium-rare) or 160° (medium), basting occasionally with marinade. Let stand 10 minutes before slicing. Transfer to a serving platter; garnish, if desired. Serve with Royal Butter. Yield: 10 servings.

ROYAL BUTTER

½ cup butter or margarine, softened
1 (8-ounce) package cream cheese,
   softened

¼ cup mayonnaise
¼ cup prepared horseradish, drained

Combine all ingredients in a medium mixing bowl; beat at medium speed of an electric mixer until blended. Serve at room temperature. Yield: 2 cups.

Potato Puff Soufflé

2 teaspoons minced onion
¼ cup butter or margarine, melted
¼ cup all-purpose flour
1 teaspoon salt

¼ teaspoon pepper
2 cups cooked, mashed potato
1 (8-ounce) carton sour cream
4 large eggs, separated

Cook onion in butter in a large skillet over medium-high heat, stirring constantly, until tender. Reduce heat to medium. Add flour, stirring until blended. Cook, stirring constantly, until thickened and bubbly. Stir in salt and pepper; remove from heat. Stir in mashed potato and sour cream.

Beat egg yolks until thick and pale. Gradually stir about one-fourth of hot mixture into yolks, and add to remaining hot mixture, stirring constantly.

Beat egg whites in a large bowl at high speed of an electric mixer until stiff peaks form; gently fold beaten egg white into potato mixture, one-third at a time. Spoon into a buttered 1½-quart soufflé dish. Bake, uncovered, at 350° for 40 minutes or until puffed and set. Serve immediately. Yield: 6 servings.

If you don't have time to prepare mashed potatoes from scratch for this recipe, use instant mashed potato flakes.

Winter Salad with Raspberry Vinaigrette

½ pound fresh spinach, washed, trimmed, and torn
1 head Bibb lettuce, torn
2 oranges, peeled and sectioned

2 Red Delicious apples, thinly sliced
1 kiwifruit, peeled and thinly sliced
½ cup chopped walnuts, toasted
Raspberry Vinaigrette

Combine first 6 ingredients in a large bowl; toss gently. Pour Raspberry Vinaigrette over spinach mixture just before serving; toss gently. Yield: 6 to 8 servings.

RASPBERRY VINAIGRETTE

½ cup vegetable oil
¼ cup raspberry vinegar
1 tablespoon honey

½ teaspoon grated orange rind
¼ teaspoon salt
⅛ teaspoon pepper

Combine all ingredients in a jar; cover tightly, and shake vigorously. Cover and chill thoroughly. Yield: about 1 cup.

Christmas Morning Brunch

Orange Streusel Muffins

Gingerbread Scones

Fresh Strawberries and Orange Slices

Baked Sausage and Eggs

Mediterranean Coffee

Serves 6

Christmas morning at last! All the shopping is done and now it's your turn to relax and enjoy the excitement. And with this make-ahead menu, you'll be spending time with your loved ones, not laboring in the kitchen. Enjoy the spiced coffee as you open presents and snack on home-made scones and muffins. Bring out the casserole after everyone has worked up an appetite opening presents.

SHOPPING LIST

Staples: all-purpose flour, baking powder, baking soda, butter or margarine, ground coffee, milk, salt, sugar, vegetable oil, Worcestershire sauce

. . . .

Herbs and Spices: ground cinnamon, cinnamon sticks, whole cloves, ground ginger, ground nutmeg

. . . .

4 fresh oranges
1 pint fresh strawberries

. . . .

1 stick unsalted butter
8 ounces sharp Cheddar cheese, shredded
4 ounces Monterey Jack cheese, shredded
7 large eggs
½ cup half-and-half
½ pint whipping cream

. . . .

¼ cup chocolate syrup
½ cup orange marmalade
⅓ cup molasses
¼ cup orange juice
½ cup chopped pecans
6 breakfast sausage links
Anise extract

. . . .

Garnish: candy canes

ORANGE STREUSEL MUFFINS

2 cups all-purpose flour
2 teaspoons baking powder
1 teaspoon salt
⅓ cup sugar
½ cup chopped pecans
1 large egg, lightly beaten
¼ cup orange juice
¼ cup milk
¼ cup vegetable oil

1 tablespoon grated orange rind
½ cup orange marmalade
1 tablespoon all-purpose flour
¼ cup sugar
½ teaspoon ground cinnamon
¼ teaspoon ground nutmeg
1 tablespoon butter or margarine,
   softened

Combine first 5 ingredients in a large bowl; make a well in center of mixture. Set dry ingredients aside.

Combine egg and next 5 ingredients; add to dry ingredients, stirring just until moistened. Spoon batter into greased muffins pans, filling two-thirds full.

Combine 1 tablespoon flour and remaining 4 ingredients; sprinkle over batter. Bake at 400° for 17 minutes or until golden. Remove from pans immediately. Yield: 15 muffins.

GINGERBREAD SCONES

2 cups all-purpose flour
2 teaspoons baking powder
¼ teaspoon baking soda
1 teaspoon ground ginger
1 teaspoon ground cinnamon

¼ cup plus 3 tablespoons unsalted
   butter
⅓ cup molasses
⅓ cup milk

Combine first 5 ingredients; cut in butter with a pastry blender until mixture is crumbly. Combine molasses and milk; add to flour mixture, stirring just until dry ingredients are moistened. Turn dough out onto a lightly floured surface, and knead lightly 4 or 5 times.

Divide dough in half; shape each portion into a ball. Pat each ball into a 5-inch circle on an ungreased baking sheet. Cut each circle into 6 wedges, using a sharp knife; do not separate wedges.

Bake at 425° for 10 to 12 minutes or until lightly browned. Serve warm. Yield: 1 dozen.

BAKED SAUSAGE AND EGGS

6 breakfast sausage links
2 cups (8 ounces) shredded sharp
  Cheddar cheese
1 tablespoon all-purpose flour
1 cup (4 ounces) shredded Monterey
  Jack cheese

6 large eggs, lightly beaten
½ cup half-and-half
1 teaspoon Worcestershire sauce

Cook sausage links according to package directions; drain on paper towels. Set sausage aside.

Combine Cheddar cheese and flour; sprinkle evenly in bottom of an ungreased 1½-quart shallow round baking dish. Sprinkle with Monterey Jack cheese, and set aside.

Combine eggs, half-and-half, and Worcestershire sauce; pour over cheese mixture. Arrange sausages on top of egg mixture in spoke fashion. Cover and chill 8 hours.

Remove from refrigerator. Let stand, covered, at room temperature 30 minutes. Bake, uncovered, at 350° for 45 minutes or until set and lightly browned. Let stand 5 minutes before serving. Yield: 6 servings.

MEDITERRANEAN COFFEE

¾ cup ground coffee
4 (3-inch) sticks cinnamon
1½ teaspoons whole cloves
8 cups water
¼ cup chocolate syrup

⅓ cup sugar
½ teaspoon anise extract
Whipped cream
Garnish: candy canes

If you like black coffee, you'll love this full-bodied brew. For a sweeter taste, increase the amount of sugar to ½ cup.

Place ground coffee, cinnamon, and cloves in the coffee filter or filter basket. Add water to coffeemaker, and brew.

Stir syrup, sugar, and anise into brewed coffee. Pour into mugs; top each with a dollop of whipped cream. Garnish, if desired. Yield: 8 cups.

Casual Entertaining

Smoked Gouda Pork Chops

Better than Grandma's Potatoes

Spinach-Apple Salad

Sweet Potato Praline Pie

Serves 8

Have an intimate gathering with friends this holiday season by inviting them over for a casual dinner. They'll marvel over the delicious pork chops topped with savory smoked gouda and exclaim that your mashed potatoes rival Grandma's anyday!

SHOPPING LIST

Staples: all-purpose flour, dark brown sugar, sugar, butter or margarine, salt, pepper, shortening, vegetable oil, white vinegar

Herbs and Spices: ground cinnamon, ground cloves, curry powder, dried dillweed, ground nutmeg, dry mustard, sweet Hungarian paprika

1 bunch fresh parsley
4 Red Delicious apples
4 small carrots
1 head fresh garlic
1 bunch green onions
4 large onions
1 small onion
3 pounds baking potatoes
3 medium-size sweet potatoes
1½ pounds fresh spinach

3 ounces smoked Gouda cheese
3 large eggs
1 (16-ounce) carton sour cream

2 cups beef broth
2½ quarts chicken broth
Chutney
1 (12-ounce) can evaporated milk
⅔ cup salted dry roasted peanuts
⅓ cup chopped pecans
⅔ cup raisins
3 tablespoons sesame seeds
8 (1-inch-thick) rib pork chops

SMOKED GOUDA PORK CHOPS

Caramelized onions and smoked Gouda create a unique combination of exquisite tastes in this pork chop dish.

1 cup all-purpose flour
1¼ teaspoons salt, divided
1¼ teaspoons pepper, divided
8 (1-inch-thick) rib pork chops
½ cup plus 1 tablespoon vegetable oil, divided
1 tablespoon plus 1 teaspoon sweet Hungarian paprika, divided
4 large onions, sliced

1 teaspoon sugar
1 tablespoon minced garlic
2 cups beef broth
¾ cup (3 ounces) shredded smoked Gouda cheese
3 tablespoons butter or margarine
¼ cup plus 1 tablespoon all-purpose flour

Combine 1 cup flour, 1 teaspoon salt, and 1 teaspoon pepper in a large heavy-duty, zip-top plastic bag. Add chops; seal bag, and shake to coat.

Heat 3 tablespoons oil in a large heavy skillet over medium-high heat until hot; add 4 chops. Cook 3 minutes on each side or until browned. Transfer to a 15- x 10- x 2-inch baking dish. Repeat procedure. Sprinkle chops evenly with 1 teaspoon paprika. Wipe skillet with a paper towel.

Heat remaining 3 tablespoons oil in skillet. Add onion; sprinkle with sugar. Cook, stirring constantly, 20 minutes or until tender and golden. Add garlic; cook 1 minute. Remove from heat. Add remaining 1 tablespoon paprika; stir well. Spoon onion over chops. Pour broth over onion mixture. Cover and bake at 350° for 45 minutes. Remove from oven; transfer chops to a platter. Pour onion mixture through a wire-mesh strainer into a 4-cup liquid measuring cup. Add enough water to broth mixture to measure 2½ cups; set aside. Return solids in strainer to baking dish; top with chops. Sprinkle with cheese. Bake 5 minutes; set aside, and keep warm.

Melt butter in a heavy saucepan over low heat; add ¼ cup plus 1 tablespoon flour, stirring until smooth. Cook 1 minute, stirring constantly. Gradually add reserved broth mixture; cook over medium heat, stirring constantly, until thickened and bubbly. Stir in remaining ¼ teaspoon salt and ¼ teaspoon pepper. Serve chops and onion with sauce. Yield: 8 servings.

BETTER THAN GRANDMA'S POTATOES

3 pounds baking potatoes, peeled
2½ quarts chicken broth
4 small carrots, scraped and cut into ½-inch pieces
1 small onion, chopped
¼ cup butter or margarine

1 teaspoon dried dillweed
1½ cups sour cream
3 tablespoons chopped fresh parsley
1 teaspoon salt
¼ teaspoon pepper
1 tablespoon butter or margarine

Combine potatoes and chicken broth in a Dutch oven; bring to a boil. Reduce heat, and simmer 15 minutes. Add carrot and onion, and simmer 20 minutes or until potatoes are tender; drain.

Combine cooked vegetables, ¼ cup butter, and dillweed in a large bowl; mash. Add sour cream and next 3 ingredients, stirring well. Spoon potato mixture into a greased 11- x 7- x 1½-inch baking dish; dot with 1 tablespoon butter. Cover and bake at 325° for 1 hour. Yield: 8 servings.

SPINACH-APPLE SALAD

⅔ cup vegetable oil
½ cup white vinegar
1 tablespoon chutney
1 teaspoon salt
1 teaspoon curry powder
1 teaspoon dry mustard
10 cups tightly packed torn fresh
    spinach

4 Red Delicious apples, diced
⅔ cup salted dry roasted peanuts
⅔ cup raisins
½ cup sliced green onions
3 tablespoons sesame seeds, toasted

Whisk together first 6 ingredients. Cover; let stand at room temperature 2 hours.
Combine spinach and remaining 5 ingredients in a bowl; toss well. Pour dressing over spinach mixture, and toss gently. Serve immediately. Yield: 8 servings.

SWEET POTATO PRALINE PIE

1⅓ cups all-purpose flour
½ teaspoon salt
½ cup shortening
3 to 4 tablespoons cold water
3 tablespoons butter or margarine,
    softened
⅓ cup firmly packed dark brown
    sugar
⅓ cup chopped pecans
3 large eggs, lightly beaten

1 cup evaporated milk
1½ cups cooked, mashed sweet
    potatoes
½ cup sugar
½ cup firmly packed dark brown
    sugar
1 teaspoon salt
1 teaspoon ground cinnamon
¼ teaspoon ground cloves
¼ teaspoon ground nutmeg

A luscious praline layer baked in the crust elevates this classic sweet potato pie to a new level.

Combine flour and ½ teaspoon salt; cut in shortening with pastry blender until mixture is crumbly. Sprinkle cold water (1 tablespoon at a time) over surface; stir with a fork until dry ingredients are moistened. Shape into a ball; cover and chill.
Roll dough into a 12-inch circle on a lightly floured surface. Place in a 10-inch pieplate; trim off excess pastry along edges. Fold edges under, and flute.
Combine butter and ⅓ cup brown sugar; stir in pecans. Press mixture over pastry shell. Bake at 425° for 5 minutes. Cool on a wire rack. Reduce oven temperature to 350°. Combine eggs and remaining 8 ingredients in a mixing bowl; beat at medium speed of an electric mixer until blended. Pour mixture over praline layer in pastry shell. Bake at 350° for 50 minutes or until set. Cool on wire rack. Yield: one 10-inch pie.

Open House

PARTY ROSEMARY PORK   COCKTAIL ROLLS

LAYERED CHEESE TORTA   CRACKERS

QUICK 'N' CHEESY COCKTAIL SWIRLS

ROCKY ROAD FUDGE BROWNIES

Serves 24

Entertaining a large crowd is easy with an open house. And to make the party flow smoothly, plan ahead. Since the torta needs to be chilled at least 8 hours, make it the day before. The Quick 'n' Cheesy Cocktail Swirls can also be made ahead and chilled up to 2 hours before baking. Take advantage of these and the other make-ahead recipes included in this menu, and you can join the party.

SHOPPING LIST

Staples: butter or margarine, mayonnaise, milk, olive oil, salt, pepper, peppercorns, vanilla extract

. . . .

Herbs and Spices. dried rosemary

. . . .

2½ cups fresh basil leaves
3 cloves garlic
1 small onion

. . . .

1 pound unsalted butter
2 (8-ounce) packages cream cheese
2 (3-ounce) packages cream cheese
Grated Parmesan cheese
1 cup refrigerated finely shredded Parmesan cheese
2 (8-ounce) cans refrigerated crescent dinner rolls

. . . .

10 slices bacon
1 (19.8-ounce) package brownie mix
2 (1-ounce) squares unsweetened chocolate
About 1½ pounds assorted crackers for torta
6 dozen cocktail rolls
1 (7.5-ounce) jar mustard with honey
Balsamic vinegar
Kosher salt
¼ cup pine nuts
1 cup chopped pecans
3 cups miniature marshmallows
1 (16-ounce) package powdered sugar
2 (3-pound) rolled boneless pork loin roasts
1 (7-ounce) jar dried tomatoes in oil

. . . .

Garnishes: fresh rosemary sprigs, fresh basil leaves

PARTY ROSEMARY PORK

2 (3-pound) rolled boneless pork loin
  roasts
⅓ cup olive oil
¼ cup dried rosemary
2 tablespoons coarsely ground
  pepper

2 tablespoons balsamic vinegar
2 teaspoons kosher salt
¾ cup mustard with honey
¾ cup mayonnaise
6 dozen cocktail rolls
Garnish: fresh rosemary sprigs

Remove strings from roast, and separate into 4 single roasts. Place roasts on a lightly greased rack in a large roasting pan. Bake, uncovered, at 350° for 30 minutes.

Combine oil and next 4 ingredients; brush over pork. Bake, uncovered, 45 more minutes or until meat thermometer inserted in thickest portion of pork registers 160°. Remove from oven, and let stand, covered, 10 minutes before slicing.

Combine mustard and mayonnaise. Cut pork into thin slices, and serve on cocktail rolls with sauce. Garnish platter, if desired. Yield: 24 appetizer servings.

LAYERED CHEESE TORTA

Dried tomatoes and fresh basil leaves create ribbons of holiday color between creamy white cheese layers in this appetizer spread.

1 (7-ounce) jar dried tomatoes in oil,
  undrained
3 cloves garlic
2½ cups loosely packed fresh basil
  leaves
1 cup refrigerated finely shredded
  Parmesan cheese
¼ cup pine nuts, toasted

⅛ teaspoon salt
⅛ teaspoon pepper
⅓ cup olive oil
2 cups unsalted butter, softened
2 (8-ounce) packages cream cheese,
  cut into 1-inch cubes
Garnishes: fresh basil leaves

Lightly grease an 8½- x 4½- x 3-inch loafpan. Line pan with plastic wrap, allowing it to extend slightly over edges of pan. Set pan aside.

Drain tomatoes, reserving 2 tablespoons oil. Position knife blade in food processor; add tomatoes and reserved oil. Process until minced. Transfer to a bowl; set aside. Wipe processor bowl with a paper towel.

Position knife blade in processor bowl. Drop garlic through food chute with processor running; process 5 seconds or until garlic is minced. Add basil and next 4 ingredients; process until basil is finely chopped. Slowly pour olive oil through food chute with processor running; process until mixture is smooth. Transfer mixture to a small bowl, and set aside. Wipe processor bowl clean with a paper towel.

Position knife blade in processor bowl; add butter. Process until light and fluffy, stopping once to scrape down sides. Slowly drop cream cheese cubes through food chute with processor running; process until smooth, stopping once to scrape down sides.

Spread 1 cup butter mixture evenly in prepared pan, smoothing with a spatula. Spread half of basil mixture over butter mixture; top with 1 cup butter mixture.

Spread tomato mixture evenly over butter mixture. Spread 1 cup butter mixture evenly over tomato mixture. Top with remaining basil mixture and remaining butter mixture, smoothing each layer to edges of pan. Cover and chill at least 8 hours or up to 24 hours.

To serve, invert pan onto a serving platter; remove plastic wrap. Garnish, if desired. Serve with crackers. Yield: 24 appetizer servings.

QUICK 'N' CHEESY COCKTAIL SWIRLS

10 slices bacon, cooked and
   crumbled
2 (3-ounce) packages cream cheese,
   softened
¼ cup finely chopped onion

2 teaspoons milk
2 (8-ounce) cans refrigerated
   crescent dinner rolls
Grated Parmesan cheese

Combine first 4 ingredients in a small bowl, stirring well; set aside.

Unroll one can of refrigerated dough; do not separate along ridges. Roll dough into a 15- x 8-inch rectangle. Spread half of cheese mixture evenly over dough, leaving ½-inch margin at edges. Roll up dough, jellyroll fashion, starting at long side; pinch seams to seal. Cut dough into ½-inch slices; place slices, cut side down, on ungreased baking sheets. Sprinkle lightly with Parmesan cheese. Repeat with other can of dough and remaining cheese mixture. Bake at 375° for 12 to 15 minutes or until golden. Serve warm. Yield: 5 dozen.

Looking for a warm appetizer that won't keep you in the kitchen while your guests entertain themselves? These can be made ahead and refrigerated up to two hours before baking.

ROCKY ROAD FUDGE BROWNIES

1 (19.8-ounce) package brownie mix
1 cup chopped pecans
3 cups miniature marshmallows
2 (1-ounce) squares unsweetened
   chocolate

⅓ cup milk
½ cup butter or margarine
1 (16-ounce) package powdered
   sugar, sifted
½ teaspoon vanilla extract

Prepare brownie mix according to package directions; stir in pecans. Spoon batter into a greased 13- x 9- x 2-inch baking pan.

Bake at 350° for 25 minutes. Remove from oven, and immediately sprinkle miniature marshmallows over hot brownies.

Combine chocolate, ⅓ cup milk, and butter in a heavy saucepan. Cook over low heat until chocolate and butter melt, stirring often.

Remove from heat. Transfer to a medium mixing bowl. Add powdered sugar and vanilla; beat at low speed of an electric mixer until smooth. (If frosting is too stiff for spreading consistency, add milk, 1 tablespoon at a time, stirring until smooth.) Spread over brownies. Cool in pan on a wire rack. Cover and chill at least 1 hour or up to 24 hours before cutting into bars. Yield: 2 dozen.

These chewy chocolate gems will disappear quickly. Bake two batches to make sure you have enough. If some happen to remain after the party, your family will love you for it.

Caroling Party

SAUTÉED SHRIMP WITH PASTA

MIXED SALAD GREENS WITH GARLIC DRESSING

PARMESAN BREADSTICKS

CHOCOLATE-RAISIN BREAD PUDDING

Serves 8

After singing stanza after stanza of your favorite carols, bring your joyful group in from the cold for a festive supper. They'll praise you over the succulent shrimp and pasta while you marvel at the simplicity of this dish. Toss the tangy dressing with salad greens for a quick accompaniment. And bet that guests will come back for more of these soft, buttery breadsticks. Then after dessert, you'll be ready to sing another round of Christmas melodies.

SHOPPING LIST

Staples: all-purpose flour, butter or margarine, honey, mayonnaise, milk, olive oil, salt, pepper, sugar, brown sugar, vanilla extract

. . . .

Herbs and Spices: garlic powder, dried parsley flakes

. . . .

2 cloves elephant garlic
2 (10-ounce) bags mixed salad greens
1 medium lemon
1 orange

. . . .

½ cup plus 2 tablespoons grated Parmesan cheese
9 large eggs
2 (½-pint) cartons whipping cream

. . . .

1 (1-pound) loaf cinnamon-raisin bread
4 ounces semisweet chocolate
2 (0.7-ounce) envelopes Italian dressing mix
2 (¼-ounce) envelopes active dry yeast
1 pound linguine or pasta of choice
3 pounds unpeeled large fresh shrimp
1 cup Irish cream liqueur
¼ cup dark rum
½ cup raisins
1 vanilla bean

SAUTÉED SHRIMP WITH PASTA

3 pounds unpeeled large fresh
  shrimp
½ cup butter or margarine

2 (0.7-ounce) envelopes Italian
  dressing mix
Hot cooked pasta

Peel shrimp, and devein, if desired.

Melt butter in a large skillet over medium heat; stir in dressing mix. Add shrimp; cook, stirring constantly, 3 to 5 minutes or until shrimp turn pink. Serve immediately over pasta. Yield: 8 servings.

GARLIC DRESSING

If any dressing is left over, use it as a marinade for meats or a topping for baked potatoes or burgers.

2 tablespoons fresh lemon juice
2 cloves elephant garlic
½ cup grated Parmesan cheese
¼ cup olive oil

3 tablespoons mayonnaise
1 teaspoon salt
½ teaspoon freshly ground pepper

Position knife blade in food processor bowl; add lemon juice and garlic. Process until garlic is finely chopped. Place garlic mixture in a small bowl; stir in cheese and remaining ingredients. Yield: 1 cup.

PARMESAN BREADSTICKS

2 (¼-ounce) envelopes active dry
  yeast
1½ cups warm water (105° to 115°),
  divided
4 cups all-purpose flour, divided
2 teaspoons salt
1½ tablespoons honey

1 large egg
½ cup butter or margarine
2 tablespoons grated Parmesan
  cheese
½ teaspoon garlic powder
½ teaspoon dried parsley flakes

Combine yeast and ½ cup warm water in a 1-cup liquid measuring cup; let stand 5 minutes. Combine 2 cups flour and salt; set aside.

Combine yeast mixture, remaining 1 cup warm water, honey, and egg in a large mixing bowl; beat at medium speed of an electric mixer until blended. Gradually add flour mixture, beating until well blended. Gradually stir in enough remaining 2 cups flour to make a soft dough.

Turn dough out onto a floured surface, and knead until smooth and elastic (6 to 8 minutes). Place in a well-greased bowl, turning to grease top. Cover and let rise in a warm place (85°), free from drafts, 15 minutes.

Combine butter and remaining 3 ingredients in a small saucepan; cook over medium heat until butter melts, stirring occasionally. Set aside.

Punch dough down; turn out onto a lightly floured surface. Roll dough into a 21-x 6½-inch rectangle. Cut dough crosswise into 21 (1-inch) strips. Twist each strip 2 times (dough will be soft). Place strips on a lightly greased baking sheet, and brush with half of butter mixture. Cover and let rise in a warm place, free from drafts, 10 minutes.

Bake at 400° for 12 to 13 minutes. Brush with remaining butter mixture; serve immediately. Yield: 21 breadsticks.

CHOCOLATE-RAISIN BREAD PUDDING

1 (1-pound) loaf cinnamon-raisin bread
4 large eggs, lightly beaten
1½ cups milk
½ cup whipping cream
½ cup firmly packed brown sugar
⅓ cup Irish cream liqueur
¼ cup dark rum
4 ounces semisweet chocolate, chopped
½ cup raisins
1 tablespoon grated orange rind
1 tablespoon vanilla extract
Crème Anglaise

Remove crust from bread; reserve crust for other uses. Cut bread into cubes, and place in a large bowl.

Combine eggs and next 5 ingredients in a medium bowl; stir in chocolate and next 3 ingredients. Pour egg mixture over bread; stir well. Cover and chill 30 minutes.

Pour into a greased 9-inch springform pan. Bake, uncovered, at 350° for 50 minutes or until a knife inserted in center comes out clean. Cool in pan 5 minutes. Carefully remove sides of springform pan; cut bread pudding into wedges. Serve warm with Crème Anglaise. Yield: 8 servings.

CRÈME ANGLAISE
1 vanilla bean
1⅓ cups whipping cream
⅔ cup milk
4 egg yolks
½ cup sugar
½ cup Irish cream liqueur

Cut a 2-inch piece of vanilla bean, reserving remaining bean for other uses. Split vanilla bean lengthwise. Combine vanilla bean, whipping cream, and milk in a medium-size heavy saucepan. Cook over medium heat, stirring constantly, until mixture reaches 185°.

Combine yolks and sugar in a bowl; beat with a wire whisk until blended. Gradually stir about one-fourth of hot mixture into yolks; add to remaining hot mixture, stirring constantly. Cook over low heat, stirring constantly, 6 minutes or until thickened. Discard vanilla bean, and stir in liqueur. Cover and chill. Yield: 2⅔ cups.

Tree-Trimming Supper

GINGER SAUSAGE BALLS

LASAGNA WITH COLORFUL PEPPERS

BUTTERED FRENCH BREAD

CHEWY CHUNKY CHOCOLATE-WALNUT COOKIES

POINSETTIA PUNCH

Serves 8

Make decorating your Christmas tree an event the family will look forward to year after year. Nibble on snappy sausage balls for starters, and then honor the occasion with this delicious lasagna that's destined to become a favorite. And don't forget punch and cookies. These sweet delights will keep everyone coming back.

SHOPPING LIST

Staples: all-purpose flour, baking soda, butter or margarine, salt, pepper, sugar, brown sugar, vanilla extract
. . . .
Herbs and Spices: crystallized ginger, fresh ginger
. . . .
1 bunch fresh parsley
4 cloves garlic
1 large onion
2 sweet red peppers
2 sweet yellow peppers
2 green peppers
. . . .
1 pound part-skim mozzarella cheese, shredded
¼ cup grated Parmesan cheese
3 large eggs
1 (12-ounce) can frozen pink lemonade concentrate
1 quart raspberry sherbet
. . . .

2 (7-ounce) milk chocolate bars
Bread for 1 cup soft breadcrumbs
1 (1-pound) loaf French bread
1 to 2 tablespoons Grand Marnier or orange juice
2 liters ginger ale
2 teaspoons prepared horseradish
12 lasagna noodles
1 (8-ounce) can tomato sauce
1 (6-ounce) can tomato paste
1½ pounds ground pork sausage
1 pound sweet Italian sausage
½ pound hot Italian sausage
1½ cups chopped walnuts or pecans
1 (10-ounce) jar apricot preserves

GINGER SAUSAGE BALLS

1½ pounds ground pork sausage
2 tablespoons chopped crystallized ginger
2 teaspoons minced fresh ginger

1 clove garlic, minced
2 large eggs, separated
1 cup soft breadcrumbs (homemade)
Marmalade-Horseradish Sauce

Combine first 4 ingredients; add egg yolks, mixing well. Beat egg whites at high speed of an electric mixer until soft peaks form. Add beaten whites and breadcrumbs to sausage mixture; mix well. Shape into 1-inch balls (about 48). Place balls on a greased rack of broiler pan. Broil 5½ inches from heat (with electric oven door partially opened) 12 minutes or until browned, turning once. Drain sausage balls; serve warm with Marmalade-Horseradish Sauce. Yield: 12 appetizer servings.

MARMALADE-HORSERADISH SAUCE

1 (10-ounce) jar apricot marmalade or preserves
2 teaspoons prepared horseradish

1 to 2 tablespoons Grand Marnier or orange juice

Combine all ingredients; cover and chill. Yield: 1 cup.

LASAGNA WITH COLORFUL PEPPERS

Italian sausage and red, green, and yellow peppers mingle among the tall cheesy layers of this extraordinary lasagna.

12 lasagna noodles, uncooked
1 pound sweet Italian sausage
½ pound hot Italian sausage
1 large onion, sliced
2 sweet red peppers, sliced
2 sweet yellow peppers, sliced
2 green peppers, sliced
3 cloves garlic, chopped

½ cup chopped fresh parsley
⅛ teaspoon pepper
1 (8-ounce) can tomato sauce
1 (6-ounce) can tomato paste
4 cups (16 ounces) shredded part-skim mozzarella cheese
¼ cup grated Parmesan cheese

Cook lasagna noodles according to package directions; drain well, and set aside.

Meanwhile, remove and discard casings from sausage. Cook sausage in a large skillet over medium heat until meat is browned, stirring until meat crumbles; drain. Add onion, sliced peppers, and garlic; cook over medium heat until vegetables are tender, stirring occasionally. Add parsley and pepper.

Combine tomato sauce and tomato paste; stir well. Spread half of tomato sauce mixture in a lightly greased 13- x 9- x 2-inch baking dish. Layer 4 lasagna noodles, half of sausage mixture, 1 cup mozzarella cheese, and 1 tablespoon Parmesan cheese. Repeat noodle, sausage, and cheese layers. Top with remaining 4 lasagna noodles; spread remaining tomato sauce mixture over noodles. Top with remaining 2 cups mozzarella cheese; sprinkle with remaining 2 tablespoons Parmesan cheese. Bake, uncovered, at 350° for 40 to 45 minutes. Let stand 15 minutes. Yield: 8 servings.

CHEWY CHUNKY CHOCOLATE-WALNUT COOKIES

1 cup butter or margarine, softened
¾ cup firmly packed brown sugar
½ cup sugar
1½ teaspoons vanilla extract
1 large egg
2¼ cups all-purpose flour
1 teaspoon baking soda

½ teaspoon salt
1½ cups coarsely chopped walnuts
   or pecans
2 (7-ounce) milk chocolate bars, cut
   into ½-inch pieces (we tested with
   Hershey's)

Beat butter at medium speed of an electric mixer until creamy; gradually add sugars, beating well. Add vanilla and egg; beat well.

Combine flour, soda, and salt; gradually add to butter mixture, beating well. Stir in walnuts and chocolate pieces.

Drop dough by rounded tablespoonfuls 2 inches apart onto ungreased cookie sheets. Bake at 375° for 10 minutes or until lightly browned. Cool slightly on cookie sheets, remove to wire racks, and let cool completely. Yield: about 4 dozen.

POINSETTIA PUNCH

1 (12-ounce) can frozen pink
   lemonade concentrate, thawed
   and undiluted

1 (2-liter) bottle ginger ale, chilled
1 quart raspberry sherbet, softened

Combine lemonade concentrate and ginger ale in a punch bowl, stirring gently. Add sherbet by heaping tablespoonfuls, and stir gently. Serve immediately. Yield: 13 cups.

Pink lemonade and raspberry sherbet revive the familiar lime sherbet punch for the holidays.

Dessert Party

CHRISTMAS CRINKLES

CHOCOLATE TRUFFLE CHEESECAKE

STRAWBERRY HOLIDAY TRIFLE

Serves 12

Most everyone loves dessert. So invite a crowd over during the holidays for this mouth-watering selection of sweet treats. Get a head start on the trifle by making the cake and custard two days before your party. On the day before, assemble the trifle, and make your cookies and cheesecake. Then all that's left to do is indulge!

SHOPPING LIST

Staples: all-purpose flour, baking powder, baking soda, butter or margarine, cornstarch, milk, salt, shortening, sugar, powdered sugar, vanilla extract
. . . .
4 pints fresh strawberries
. . . .
¼ cup buttermilk
4 (8-ounce) packages cream cheese
10 large eggs
1 (8-ounce) carton sour cream
1 (16-ounce) carton sour cream
2 (½-pint) cartons whipping cream
. . . .
¾ cup sliced almonds
1 (12-ounce) package semisweet chocolate morsels
1 (4-ounce) bar white chocolate
1½ cups crushed cream-filled chocolate sandwich cookies
Hard peppermint candy
⅓ cup seedless raspberry preserves
¾ cup strawberry wine
. . . .
Garnishes: fresh mint sprigs, fresh raspberries

CHRISTMAS CRINKLES

1 (4-ounce) bar white chocolate,
  coarsely chopped
⅓ cup butter or margarine, softened
1½ cups sugar, divided
¼ cup buttermilk
1 teaspoon vanilla extract
1 large egg

2½ cups all-purpose flour
½ teaspoon baking soda
¼ teaspoon salt
½ cup (3 ounces) semisweet
  chocolate morsels
1 tablespoon shortening
Crushed hard peppermint candy

Melt white chocolate in a saucepan over low heat, stirring constantly. Remove from heat. Beat butter at medium speed of an electric mixer until creamy. Gradually add 1 cup sugar; beat well. Add melted white chocolate, buttermilk, vanilla, and egg; beat well. Combine flour, soda, and salt; gradually add to batter, beating well. Cover; chill 1 hour. Shape dough into 1-inch balls; roll balls in remaining ½ cup sugar. Place 2 inches apart on ungreased cookie sheets. Bake at 375° for 8 minutes or until bottoms of cookies are lightly browned. Cool slightly on cookie sheets. Remove to wire racks. Melt chocolate morsels and shortening in a saucepan over low heat, stirring constantly. Drizzle over cookies; sprinkle with candy. Yield: 5 dozen.

CHOCOLATE TRUFFLE CHEESECAKE

For ease, look for packaged crushed sandwich cookies in the cake mix section of your local supermarket.

1½ cups crushed cream-filled chocolate sandwich cookies (21 cookies)
¼ cup butter or margarine, melted
4 (8-ounce) packages cream cheese,
  softened and divided
1½ cups sugar, divided
3 large eggs
1 (8-ounce) carton sour cream
2 teaspoons vanilla extract, divided

1 cup (6 ounces) semisweet chocolate
  morsels, melted
⅓ cup seedless raspberry preserves
1 (16-ounce) carton sour cream
½ cup (3 ounces) semisweet
  chocolate morsels
¼ cup whipping cream
Garnishes: whipped cream, fresh
  raspberries, mint sprigs

Combine cookie crumbs and butter in a bowl. Firmly press mixture in bottom of a 10-inch springform pan. Bake at 400° for 8 minutes; cool in pan on a wire rack.

Beat 3 packages cream cheese at medium speed of an electric mixer until creamy. Gradually add 1¼ cups sugar, beating well. Add eggs, one at a time, beating after each addition. Stir in 1 (8-ounce) carton sour cream and 1 teaspoon vanilla.

Combine remaining package cream cheese, melted chocolate morsels, and preserves in a bowl; stir well. Spoon two-thirds of vanilla batter into prepared crust. Drop chocolate mixture by rounded tablespoonfuls over batter; pour remaining batter over chocolate mixture. Bake at 325° for 1 hour and 20 minutes or until almost set. (Cheesecake will rise above pan.) Increase oven temperature to 375°.

Combine 16-ounce carton sour cream, remaining ¼ cup sugar, and remaining 1 teaspoon vanilla; spread over cheesecake. Bake 5 minutes. Cool in pan on a wire rack.

Cover and chill 8 hours. To serve, remove sides of pan; slice cheesecake. Combine ½ cup chocolate morsels and whipping cream in a saucepan; cook and stir over low heat until chocolate melts. Drizzle over slices. Garnish, if desired. Yield: 12 servings.

STRAWBERRY HOLIDAY TRIFLE

4 pints strawberries, rinsed and hulled
3 tablespoons sugar
Custard
¾ cup sliced almonds, divided

Sponge Cake, cut into 1-inch cubes
¾ cup strawberry wine
Whipped cream
Garnish: 1 whole strawberry, sliced

Coarsely chop enough berries to measure 4 cups. Place in bowl, and stir in sugar; set aside. Spoon 1 cup Custard on bottom of a 12-cup trifle bowl. Sprinkle with ¼ cup almonds. Layer half of cake cubes over custard; brush cake with half of wine. Spoon 2 cups berries over cake layer; top with 1 cup Custard. Repeat layers; top with remaining Custard. Cover and chill. Top with whipped cream; sprinkle with remaining almonds. Garnish, if desired. Yield: 15 servings.

CUSTARD

⅔ cup sugar
2 tablespoons cornstarch
¼ teaspoon salt
2 cups milk

4 egg yolks, lightly beaten
2 tablespoons butter or margarine
1½ teaspoons vanilla extract
1 cup whipping cream, whipped

Whisk together first 4 ingredients in a saucepan. Cook over medium heat, stirring constantly, until thickened and bubbly. Stir about one-fourth of hot mixture into egg yolks; add to remaining hot mixture, stirring constantly. Cook over medium heat, stirring constantly, 2 minutes. Remove from heat; add butter and vanilla, stirring until butter melts. Cover with plastic wrap, gently pressing it onto surface; chill. Fold whipped cream into custard mixture. Yield: 3½ cups.

SPONGE CAKE

2 large eggs
1 cup sugar
1 cup all-purpose flour
1 teaspoon baking powder

¼ teaspoon salt
½ cup milk
2 tablespoons butter or margarine
1 teaspoon vanilla extract

Beat eggs at high speed of an electric mixer 3 minutes or until thick and pale. Gradually add sugar; beat 4 minutes. Combine flour, baking powder, and salt; gradually fold into batter. Combine milk and butter in a saucepan; cook over low heat until butter melts. Gradually stir milk mixture and vanilla into batter. Pour into two greased and floured 8-inch round cakepans. Bake at 350° for 16 minutes or until a wooden pick inserted in center comes out clean. Cool on wire racks 10 minutes. Remove from pans; cool completely on wire racks. Yield: 2 (8-inch) cake layers.

New Year's Eve Dinner

BLACK-EYED PEA AND PEPPER CAVIAR   CHIPS

GOLDEN GLAZED HAM

SPINACH-VEGETABLE COUSCOUS

ORANGE BLOSSOM CHEESECAKE

CHAMPAGNE

Serves 12

Celebrate a new year by serving this lucky menu. It contains the key ingredients to satisfy the Southern customs that will make the next year a giant success. Black-eyed peas in the appetizer will ensure your share of good luck. And the "greens" (spinach) in the couscous casserole will bring financial rewards. The ham? It's just to keep things Southern. Enjoy a little bubbly with the decadent cheesecake as you receive the new year.

SHOPPING LIST

Staples: butter or margarine, Dijon mustard, honey, olive oil, salt, pepper, sugar, brown sugar, vanilla extract

Herbs and Spices: ground cinnamon, ground cumin, ground ginger, ground turmeric

1 head fresh garlic
1 large piece fresh ginger (⅓ cup sliced)
3 medium carrots
2 lemons or ¼ cup bottled lemon juice
1 large onion
1 small purple onion
1 sweet yellow pepper
1 green pepper
2 jalapeño peppers
1 small yellow squash
1 small zucchini
2½ ounces spinach
1 large and 2 medium tomatoes
8 oranges

4 (8-ounce) packages cream cheese
4 large eggs

½ cup slivered almonds
2 (12-ounce) cans beer
½ cup bourbon
Champagne for 12
2 (14½-ounce) cans chicken broth
Corn chips or tortilla chips for 12
6 ounces white chocolate
3 cups gingersnap crumbs
8 ounces couscous
½ cup pitted dates
½ cup golden raisins
1 (7-pound) fully cooked ham half
2 (15-ounce) cans black-eyed peas
1 (15-ounce) can black-eyed peas with jalapeño peppers
1 (2-ounce) jar diced pimiento
1 cup Italian dressing

BLACK-EYED PEA AND PEPPER CAVIAR

If you'd like to "lighten" this colorful dip, substitute a fat-free Italian dressing for the regular dressing.

2 (15-ounce) cans black-eyed peas, rinsed and drained
1 (15-ounce) can black-eyed peas with jalapeño peppers, rinsed and drained
2 medium tomatoes, seeded and chopped
1 cup Italian dressing
¾ cup chopped onion

½ cup chopped sweet yellow pepper
½ cup chopped green pepper
¼ to ¾ cup seeded, chopped jalapeño pepper
1 (2-ounce) jar diced pimiento, drained
1½ teaspoons minced garlic
½ teaspoon ground cumin
½ teaspoon pepper

Combine all ingredients in a large bowl, stirring well. Cover and chill at least 2 hours. Serve dip with large corn chips or tortilla chips. Yield: 8 cups.

GOLDEN GLAZED HAM

Leftovers from this recipe are yummy straight from the fridge.

1 (7-pound) fully cooked ham half
2 cups firmly packed brown sugar, divided
2 (12-ounce) cans beer

2 tablespoons honey
2 tablespoons Dijon mustard
½ cup bourbon

Place ham, fat side up, in a deep roasting pan. Press 1 cup brown sugar onto all sides of ham. Pour beer into pan. Insert meat thermometer into ham, making sure it does not touch fat or bone. Cover and bake at 325° for 30 minutes. Remove 2 cups drippings from pan.

Combine remaining 1 cup brown sugar, honey, mustard, and bourbon in a saucepan; cook over medium heat, stirring constantly, until sugar melts. Baste ham with sugar mixture. Return ham to oven; bake, uncovered, 1 hour or until meat thermometer registers 140°, basting with reserved drippings and sugar mixture every 10 minutes. Let stand 10 minutes before slicing. Yield: 14 servings.

SPINACH-VEGETABLE COUSCOUS

¼ cup olive oil
1½ teaspoons ground ginger
1½ teaspoons ground turmeric
1½ teaspoons ground cinnamon
2 (14½-ounce) cans chicken broth
1⅓ cups couscous, uncooked (about 8 ounces)
½ cup golden raisins
½ cup pitted dates, diced
½ cup blanched almonds, toasted

3 medium carrots, scraped and diced
1 large tomato, diced
1 small yellow squash, diced
1 small zucchini, diced
1 small purple onion, chopped
3 cups spinach leaves, rolled and sliced (about 2½ ounces)
½ cup olive oil
¼ cup lemon juice
¼ teaspoon salt

Combine first 5 ingredients in a Dutch oven; bring to a boil. Add couscous; cook 2 minutes or until most of liquid is absorbed, stirring often. Remove from heat; stir in raisins and dates. Cover and let stand 15 minutes.

Combine almonds and next 6 ingredients in a large bowl. Combine ½ cup oil, lemon juice, and salt in a jar; cover tightly, and shake vigorously. Pour oil mixture over almond mixture; toss well. Add couscous mixture; toss well. Serve immediately or chill slightly. Yield: 12 servings.

ORANGE BLOSSOM CHEESECAKE

3 cups gingersnap crumbs
⅓ cup butter or margarine, melted
2 teaspoons grated orange rind
1½ cups fresh orange juice
⅓ cup unpeeled and thinly sliced
    fresh ginger
4 (8-ounce) packages cream cheese,
    softened
⅔ cup sugar

6 ounces white chocolate, melted
4 large eggs
2 tablespoons grated orange rind
1 tablespoon vanilla extract
3 cups water
1½ cups sugar
2 oranges, unpeeled and cut into
    very thin slices

To make slicing this cheesecake easier, cut the oranges for decorating the top into the thinnest possible slices.

Combine first 3 ingredients in a bowl; stir well. Firmly press crumb mixture on bottom and up sides of a 9-inch springform pan. Chill.

Combine orange juice and ginger in a saucepan; bring to a boil. Reduce heat, and simmer 20 to 30 minutes or until reduced to 3 tablespoons. Pour mixture through a wire-mesh strainer into a small bowl, discarding ginger. Set orange juice mixture aside.

Beat cream cheese at medium speed of an electric mixer until creamy. Add ⅔ cup sugar, beating well. Add strained orange juice mixture, and beat well. With mixer running, add chocolate in a steady stream, beating until blended. Add eggs, one at a time, beating after each addition. Stir in 2 tablespoons orange rind and vanilla. Pour batter into prepared pan.

Bake at 300° for 1 hour and 25 minutes. Turn oven off, and leave cheesecake in oven 4 hours. (Do not open oven door.). Let cool to room temperature in pan on a wire rack; cover and chill at least 8 hours.

Cover a wire rack with wax paper; set aside. Combine water and 1½ cups sugar in a large skillet; cook over medium heat until sugar dissolves, stirring often. Reduce heat to medium-low; simmer 3 minutes. Add orange slices, one at a time, and simmer 45 minutes. Turn orange slices, and simmer 45 more minutes or until tender and translucent. Arrange orange slices in a single layer on prepared rack. Let dry 1 hour.

Carefully remove sides of springform pan. Overlap orange slices in a decorative pattern on top of cheesecake. Yield: 12 servings.

Next-Day Turkey Curry
(menu on following page)

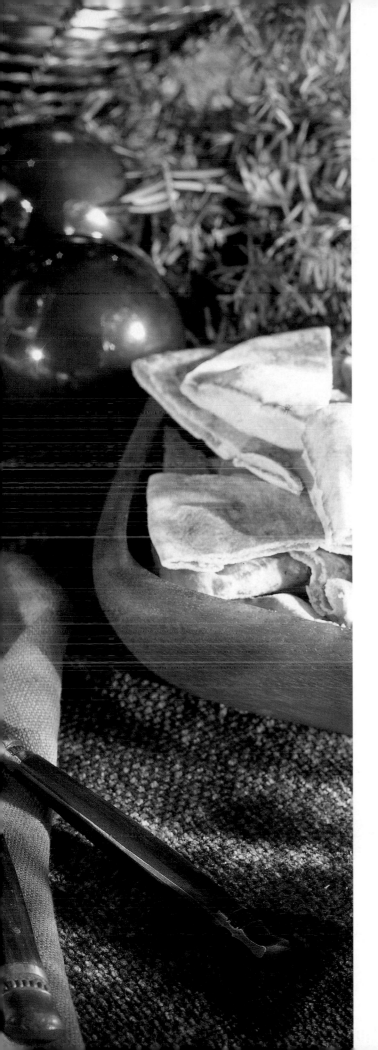

Easy
Everyday
Meals

Life goes on amid the hustle and bustle of the holidays. This chapter provides 10 everyday menu ideas that leave you time to celebrate this season of joy. Turn to these recipes when time is tight. They provide ease for weeknight family meals or small gatherings among friends. You'll also find suggested meal accompaniments as well as a shopping list to make planning a breeze.

Turkey Encore

NEXT-DAY TURKEY CURRY • RICE

PITA BREAD • TOFFEE ICE CREAM PIE

Serves 4

NEXT-DAY TURKEY CURRY

¾ cup raisins
¼ cup plus 2 tablespoons butter or
  margarine, melted
2 medium onions, chopped
Curry Spice
1 tablespoon cornstarch
1 cup chicken broth

3 cups chopped cooked turkey
1 (10-ounce) package frozen
  English peas, thawed
4 cups hot cooked rice
1 (8-ounce) carton plain low-fat
  yogurt
1 cup whole-berry cranberry sauce

Cook raisins in melted butter in a large skillet over medium-high heat, stirring constantly, 2 minutes. Remove raisins to a bowl, using a slotted spoon. Set aside.

Add onion to skillet; cook over medium-high heat, stirring constantly, until tender. Stir in Curry Spice. Combine cornstarch and broth; add to onion mixture. Cook, stirring constantly, until mixture is thickened and bubbly. Add turkey; cook 5 minutes. Stir in peas; cook just until heated.

Spoon turkey mixture over rice. Sprinkle with raisins. Serve with yogurt and cranberry sauce. Yield: 4 servings.

CURRY SPICE

2 tablespoons curry powder
½ teaspoon dry mustard or
  mustard seeds

½ teaspoon ground cumin
½ teaspoon ground ginger
¼ teaspoon ground cinnamon

Combine all ingredients. Yield: 2½ tablespoons.

TOFFEE ICE CREAM PIE

1⅓ cups vanilla wafer crumbs
¼ cup butter or margarine, melted
1 quart vanilla ice cream, softened
½ cup almond brickle chips
⅔ cup sugar

½ cup evaporated milk
2 tablespoons butter or margarine
2 tablespoons light corn syrup
Dash of salt
½ cup almond brickle chips

Combine wafer crumbs and melted butter; press firmly in bottom and up sides of a 9-inch pieplate. Bake at 375° for 8 minutes. Cool completely.

Combine softened ice cream and ½ cup brickle chips; spoon into prepared crust. Cover and freeze until firm.

Combine sugar and next 4 ingredients in a small saucepan; bring to a boil over low heat, stirring constantly. Cook 1 minute. Remove from heat, and stir in ½ cup brickle chips. Let sauce cool, stirring occasionally. Serve sauce with pie. Yield: one 9-inch pie.

This recipe offers a nice twist for leftover turkey. See it on page 52.

See it on page 52.

SHOPPING LIST

Staples: butter or margarine, cornstarch, light corn syrup, salt, sugar

Herbs and Spices: ground cinnamon, ground cumin, curry powder, ground ginger, dry mustard

2 medium onions

1 (10-ounce) package frozen English peas
1 quart vanilla ice cream
1 (8-ounce) carton plain low-fat yogurt

1 (7½-ounce) package almond brickle chips
1⅓ cups vanilla wafer crumbs
1 cup chicken broth
1 (16-ounce) can whole-berry cranberry sauce
1 (5-ounce) can evaporated milk
4 (6-inch) pita bread rounds
¾ cup raisins
4 cups cooked rice
3 cups chopped cooked turkey

Cozy Sunday Supper

Oven-Baked Stew

Easy Cheddar Biscuits

Serves 8

OVEN-BAKED STEW

2 pounds top round steak, cut into
   1-inch pieces
8 stalks celery, cut into ¾-inch pieces
5 small round red potatoes,
   quartered
4 large carrots, scraped and cut into
   ¾-inch pieces
2 cups chopped onion

1 (7-ounce) can sliced mushrooms,
   drained
¼ cup plus 1 tablespoon quick-
   cooking tapioca, uncooked
1 teaspoon sugar
½ teaspoon salt
½ teaspoon pepper
3 cups tomato juice

 This hearty stew is perfect for a simple supper. It simmers in the oven five hours, leaving you plenty of time to finish holiday gift wrapping.

Combine all ingredients in a roaster, stirring well. Cover and bake at 250° for 5 hours. Yield: 12 cups.

EASY CHEDDAR BISCUITS

1½ cups all-purpose flour
1 tablespoon baking powder
½ teaspoon salt
1 tablespoon sugar

1 cup (4 ounces) shredded sharp
   Cheddar cheese
⅓ cup shortening
½ cup milk

Position knife blade in food processor bowl; add first 4 ingredients. Pulse 4 or 5 times or until mixture is blended. Add cheese and shortening; pulse 4 or 5 times or until mixture is crumbly. Add milk, and pulse just until mixture forms a dough.

Turn dough out onto a lightly floured surface; shape into a ball. Pat to ¾-inch thickness. Cut with a 2-inch round biscuit cutter. Place biscuits on an ungreased baking sheet. Bake at 425° for 12 minutes or until golden. Yield: 12 biscuits.

SHOPPING LIST

Staples: all-purpose flour, baking powder, milk, salt, pepper, shortening, sugar
. . . .
4 large carrots
1 bunch celery
2 large onions
5 small round red
   potatoes
. . . .
4 ounces sharp Cheddar
   cheese, shredded
. . . .
1 (7-ounce) can sliced
   mushrooms
2 pounds top round steak
¼ cup plus 1 tablespoon
   quick-cooking tapioca
3 cups tomato juice

Holiday Comfort Food

SIMPLE SALISBURY STEAK • MASHED POTATOES

BROCCOLI CASSEROLE • STORE-BOUGHT BISCUITS

Serves 6

SIMPLE SALISBURY STEAK

1 (10¾-ounce) can cream of
   mushroom soup, undiluted and
   divided
1 pound ground beef
⅓ cup fine, dry breadcrumbs
   (store-bought)

¼ cup finely chopped onion
1 large egg, beaten
⅓ cup milk
1½ cups sliced fresh mushrooms

Combine ¼ cup soup, beef, and next 3 ingredients in a large bowl; stir well.
Shape mixture into 6 patties.

Cook patties in a large skillet over medium heat 6 minutes on each side or until
done. Remove patties, discarding drippings in skillet. Combine remaining soup,
milk, and mushrooms in skillet; cook until thoroughly heated. Serve mushroom
gravy over steak. Yield: 6 servings.

BROCCOLI CASSEROLE

2 (10-ounce) packages frozen
   chopped broccoli
1 (10¾ ounce) can cream of
   celery soup, undiluted
1 (8-ounce) can sliced water
   chestnuts, drained

1 (2.8-ounce) can French fried
   onions
¾ cup (3 ounces) shredded
   Cheddar cheese

Cook broccoli according to package directions; drain.

Combine broccoli, soup, water chestnuts, and onions in a small bowl; stir well.
Spoon into a lightly greased 1½-quart baking dish. Cover and bake at 350° for
20 to 25 minutes. Uncover and sprinkle with cheese; bake 2 to 3 more minutes
or until cheese melts. Yield: 6 to 8 servings.

SHOPPING LIST

Staples: butter or
   margarine, milk, salt,
   pepper (for mashed
   potatoes)
. . . .
1½ cups sliced fresh
   mushrooms
1 onion
2 pounds potatoes for
   mashing
. . . .
Biscuits
3 ounces Cheddar cheese,
   shredded
1 large egg
2 (10-ounce) packages
   frozen chopped
   broccoli
. . . .
1 pound ground beef
⅓ cup fine, dry
   breadcrumbs
1 (10¾-ounce) can
   cream of mushroom
   soup
1 (10¾-ounce) can
   cream of celery soup
1 (8-ounce) can sliced
   water chestnuts
1 (2.8-ounce) can French
   fried onions

Company Fare

Sirloin Tips with Garlic Butter • Rice

Steamed Zucchini and Yellow Squash

Fast Fudge Pots de Crème

Serves 6

Sirloin Tips with Garlic Butter

2 cups butter, softened
4 cloves garlic, minced
¼ cup dry white wine
1 tablespoon chopped fresh parsley
¼ teaspoon freshly ground pepper
1 large onion, sliced
1 (8-ounce) package sliced fresh
   mushrooms

1½ pounds sirloin steak, cut into
   1-inch pieces
½ teaspoon salt
¼ teaspoon pepper
2 tablespoons dry sherry
6 cups hot cooked rice

Combine first 5 ingredients; stir garlic butter well.

Melt 3 tablespoons garlic butter in a large skillet over medium-high heat. Add onion, and cook 3 minutes or until golden. Add mushrooms, and cook, stirring constantly, 4 minutes or until tender. Remove onion mixture from skillet. Set aside.

Sprinkle steak with salt and pepper. Melt 3 tablespoons garlic butter in skillet over medium-high heat; add steak. Cook 5 minutes or to desired degree of doneness, stirring constantly. Return onion mixture to skillet. Stir in sherry. Cook, stirring constantly, until thoroughly heated. Serve over rice. Yield: 6 servings.

Note: To chill butter in logs, spoon butter mixture onto a sheet of wax paper. Wrap in wax paper, and chill at least 30 minutes or until slightly firm. Roll butter in wax paper, back and forth, to make a log. Chill up to 2 days. You can also freeze butter logs up to 1 month.

Fast Fudge Pots de Crème

1 (3.4-ounce) package chocolate-
   flavored pudding mix
2 cups milk

1 cup (6 ounces) semisweet
   chocolate morsels

Combine pudding mix and milk in a saucepan; stir mixture well. Cook, stirring constantly, over medium heat until mixture comes to a boil; remove from heat. Add chocolate morsels, stirring until chocolate melts.

Spoon mixture evenly into eight 4-ounce pots de crème cups or soufflé cups. Serve warm or chilled. Yield: 8 servings.

This recipe makes more than enough savory garlic butter for this dish. Spoon some of the extra atop fresh squash to accompany the meal, and roll remaining butter into logs to chill or freeze for other uses.

SHOPPING LIST

Staples: butter, milk, salt, pepper
. . . .
1 tablespoon chopped fresh parsley
4 cloves garlic
1 large onion
1 (8-ounce) package sliced fresh mushrooms
1 pound fresh zucchini
1 pound fresh yellow squash
. . . .
1 (3.4-ounce) package chocolate-flavored pudding mix
1 (6-ounce) package semisweet chocolate morsels
6 cups cooked rice
2 tablespoons dry sherry
¼ cup dry white wine
1½ pounds sirloin steak

Family Favorites

10-MINUTE STROGANOFF · DEVILED CARROTS

FRENCH BREAD

Serves 6

10-MINUTE STROGANOFF

1½ pounds ground beef
1 (8-ounce) package sliced fresh
    mushrooms
1 large onion, thinly sliced
1 (16-ounce) carton sour cream

1 (10¾-ounce) can cream of
    mushroom soup, undiluted
Garlic salt and pepper to taste
    (optional)
Hot cooked egg noodles or rice

Brown beef in a large skillet, stirring until it crumbles; drain and set aside. Add mushrooms and onion to skillet; cook over medium-high heat, stirring constantly, 5 minutes or until tender. Add ground beef, sour cream, and soup; cook over medium heat 5 minutes or until thoroughly heated, stirring occasionally. If desired, stir in garlic salt and pepper to taste. Serve immediately over noodles. Yield: 6 servings.

DEVILED CARROTS

12 large carrots, scraped (about 1½
    pounds)
¾ cup butter or margarine, melted
3 tablespoons brown sugar

1 tablespoon dry mustard
3 drops of hot sauce
¾ teaspoon salt
Freshly ground pepper to taste

Cut carrots into 3-inch pieces, and quarter. Cook carrot in butter in a large skillet over medium-high heat 5 minutes, stirring constantly. Stir in brown sugar and remaining ingredients; cook 5 minutes or until tender. Serve immediately. Yield: 6 servings.

SHOPPING LIST

Staples: butter or
    margarine, brown
    sugar, hot sauce, salt,
    pepper
. . . .
Herbs and Spices: garlic
    salt (optional), dry
    mustard
. . . .
12 large carrots (1½
    pounds)
1 (8-ounce) package
    sliced fresh
    mushrooms
1 large onion
. . . .
1 (16-ounce) carton sour
    cream
. . . .
1½ pounds ground beef
French bread
1 (10¾-ounce) can cream
    of mushroom soup
12 ounces medium egg
    noodles

A Holiday Fortune

EGG DROP SOUP • ORIENTAL CHOPS AND RICE

BUTTERED STEAMED SNOW PEAS • FORTUNE COOKIES

Serves 4

EGG DROP SOUP

3½ cups chicken broth
2 large eggs, beaten
1 cup sliced fresh mushrooms
¼ cup chopped water chestnuts
¼ cup coarsely chopped fresh snow
   pea pods
1 tablespoon soy sauce
½ cup bean sprouts (optional)

Bring chicken broth to a boil in a large saucepan. Gradually add eggs, stirring mixture well.

Stir in mushrooms and remaining ingredients, including bean sprouts, if desired; reduce heat to low, and cook until thoroughly heated. Yield: 4 cups.

Here's a quick version of the trademark soup many Chinese restaurants serve.

ORIENTAL CHOPS AND RICE

4 (1¼-inch) bone-in pork loin
   chops
¾ teaspoon salt, divided
½ teaspoon pepper
½ teaspoon ground ginger, divided
1 tablespoon vegetable oil
1 cup long-grain rice, uncooked
2 cups water
2 tablespoons soy sauce
½ cup sliced green onions
½ cup chopped celery
½ cup chopped green pepper

Sprinkle chops with ¼ teaspoon salt, pepper, and ¼ teaspoon ginger. Heat oil in a large skillet; add chops, and brown in oil. Add rice, water, remaining ½ teaspoon salt, remaining ¼ teaspoon ginger, and soy sauce; stir well. Cover, reduce heat, and simmer 20 minutes. Add green onions, celery, and green pepper; cover and simmer 10 more minutes. Yield: 4 servings.

SHOPPING LIST

Staples: butter, salt,
  pepper, soy sauce,
  vegetable oil
. . . .
Herbs and Spices: ground
  ginger
. . . .
½ cup bean sprouts
  (optional)
½ cup chopped celery
1 cup sliced fresh
  mushrooms
1 bunch green onions
1 green pepper
1¼ pounds fresh snow
  pea pods
. . . .
2 large eggs
. . . .
3½ cups chicken broth
¼ cup chopped water
  chestnuts
4 (1¼-inch) bone-in pork
  loin chops
1 cup uncooked long-
  grain rice
Fortune cookies (from
  supermarket or
  Chinese restaurant)

Gathering for Friends

PRALINE CHICKEN • ROSEMARY ROASTED POTATOES

STEAMED GREEN BEANS

Serves 6

PRALINE CHICKEN

2 teaspoons Creole seasoning
6 skinned and boned chicken breast
   halves
¼ cup butter, melted

1 tablespoon vegetable oil
⅓ cup maple syrup
2 tablespoons brown sugar
1 cup chopped pecans, toasted

Sprinkle Creole seasoning on both sides of chicken. Cook chicken in butter and oil in a large skillet over medium heat 4 to 5 minutes on each side or until done. Remove chicken, reserving drippings in skillet. Place chicken on a serving platter; set aside, and keep warm.

Add maple syrup and sugar to drippings in skillet; bring to a boil. Stir in pecans, and cook 1 minute or until thoroughly heated. Spoon pecan mixture over chicken. Yield: 6 servings.

ROSEMARY ROASTED POTATOES

2 pounds round red potatoes,
   unpeeled and quartered
2 cloves garlic, minced
¼ teaspoon salt

½ teaspoon dried thyme
1 tablespoon olive oil
2 teaspoons chopped fresh rosemary
⅛ teaspoon pepper

Combine all ingredients in a large heavy-duty, zip-top plastic bag or large bowl. Seal bag, and shake well to coat. Arrange potato in a well-greased 13- x 9- x 2-inch baking dish. Bake, uncovered, at 450° for 40 minutes or until potato is tender, stirring occasionally. Yield: 6 servings.

SHOPPING LIST

Staples: brown sugar, butter, salt, pepper, olive oil, vegetable oil
. . . .
Herbs and Spices: Creole seasoning, dried thyme
. . . .
2 teaspoons chopped fresh rosemary
2 pounds fresh green beans
2 cloves garlic
2 pounds round red potatoes
. . . .
6 skinned and boned chicken breast halves
1 cup chopped pecans
⅓ cup maple syrup

Merry Weeknight Menu

PARMESAN PORK TENDERLOIN

CRUNCHY CELERY CASSEROLE • STEAMED ASPARAGUS

Serves 4

PARMESAN PORK TENDERLOIN

3 tablespoons Italian-seasoned breadcrumbs (store-bought)
1 tablespoon grated Parmesan cheese
1 teaspoon salt
⅛ teaspoon pepper

1 (1-pound) pork tenderloin, cut into 1-inch-thick slices
1 small onion, chopped
1 clove garlic, minced
2 tablespoons vegetable oil

Combine first 4 ingredients; stir well, and set aside.

Place pork between two sheets of heavy-duty plastic wrap; flatten to ½-inch thickness, using a meat mallet or rolling pin.

Dredge pork in breadcrumb mixture, coating well. Cook pork, onion, and garlic in hot oil in a large skillet over medium heat about 10 minutes or until pork is done, turning once. Yield: 4 servings.

CRUNCHY CELERY CASSEROLE

4 cups diced celery
¼ cup butter or margarine, melted and divided
1 (10¾-ounce) can cream of chicken soup, undiluted
1 (8-ounce) can sliced water chestnuts, drained

1 (2-ounce) jar diced pimiento, drained
½ cup soft breadcrumbs (homemade)
¼ cup sliced almonds

Cook celery in 2 tablespoons butter in a large skillet over medium-high heat, stirring constantly, 2 minutes or until crisp-tender.

Combine celery, soup, water chestnuts, and pimiento; stir well. Spoon into a greased 1½-quart casserole.

Combine breadcrumbs and remaining 2 tablespoons butter. Sprinkle evenly over celery mixture; top with almonds. Bake, uncovered, at 350° for 25 to 30 minutes or until bubbly. Yield: 6 servings.

SHOPPING LIST

Staples: butter or margarine, grated Parmesan cheese, salt, pepper, vegetable oil
. . . .
1¼ pounds fresh asparagus
1 bunch celery
1 clove garlic
1 small onion
. . . .
¼ cup sliced almonds
3 tablespoons Italian-seasoned breadcrumbs
Bread for ½ cup soft breadcrumbs
1 (1-pound) pork tenderloin
1 (10¾-ounce) can cream of chicken soup
1 (2-ounce) jar diced pimiento
1 (8-ounce) can sliced water chestnuts

After-Shopping Ease

Ham Steak in Orange Sauce

Baked Sweet Potatoes • Broccoli Cornbread

Serves 4

Ham Steak in Orange Sauce

1 (1-pound) center-cut ham slice (¾ inch thick)
¾ cup orange juice
½ cup firmly packed brown sugar
1 tablespoon cornstarch
⅛ teaspoon ground ginger
⅛ teaspoon ground cloves

Place ham slice in an 11- x 7- x 1½-inch baking dish. Combine orange juice and remaining 4 ingredients; pour over ham. Microwave, uncovered, at HIGH 4 minutes. Baste ham with sauce; microwave at HIGH 4 more minutes. Yield: 4 servings.

Here's a kid pleaser that'll even delight the cook—this ham is on the table in less than 15 minutes.

Broccoli Cornbread

1 (10-ounce) package frozen chopped broccoli, thawed
1 (8½-ounce) package corn muffin mix
4 large eggs, lightly beaten
¾ cup small-curd cottage cheese
½ cup butter or margarine, melted
⅓ cup chopped onion
1 teaspoon salt

Drain broccoli well, pressing between layers of paper towels.
Combine corn muffin mix and remaining 5 ingredients; stir well. Stir in broccoli.
Pour into a greased 13- x 9- x 2-inch baking pan. Bake at 400° for 20 to 25 minutes or until golden. Let cool slightly, and cut into squares. Yield: 12 servings.

SHOPPING LIST

Staples: brown sugar, butter or margarine, cornstarch, salt
. . . .
Herbs and Spices: ground cloves, ground ginger
. . . .
1 small onion
4 medium-size sweet potatoes
. . . .
¾ cup small-curd cottage cheese
4 large eggs
¾ cup orange juice
1 (10-ounce) package frozen chopped broccoli
. . . .
1 (8½-ounce) package corn muffin mix
1 (1-pound) center-cut ham slice (¾ inch thick)

Fisherman's Holiday

ORANGE ROUGHY PARMESAN • ALMOND-TOPPED RICE

GREEN PEAS • QUICK AND EASY TORTE

Serves 4 to 6

ORANGE ROUGHY PARMESAN

2 pounds orange roughy fillets
2 tablespoons lemon juice
½ cup grated Parmesan cheese
¼ cup butter or margarine,
    softened

3 tablespoons mayonnaise
3 tablespoons chopped green onions
¼ teaspoon salt
⅛ teaspoon freshly ground pepper
Dash of hot sauce

Place fillets on a greased rack of broiler pan; place rack in broiler pan. Brush fillets with lemon juice, and let stand at room temperature 10 minutes.

Combine Parmesan cheese and remaining 6 ingredients; set aside.

Broil fillets 8 inches from heat (with electric oven door partially opened) 8 minutes. Spread Parmesan cheese mixture evenly over 1 side of fillets. Broil 5 more minutes or until fish flakes easily when tested with a fork. Yield: 4 to 6 servings.

QUICK AND EASY TORTE

1 (10.75 ounce) loaf pound cake
1 teaspoon instant coffee granules
1 teaspoon hot water

1 (8 ounce) carton sour cream
1 cup (6 ounces) semisweet
    chocolate morsels, melted

Slice pound cake horizontally into 5 layers; set aside.

Combine coffee granules and water in a medium bowl, stirring until granules dissolve. Add sour cream and melted chocolate to coffee mixture, stirring until blended. Spread chocolate mixture between layers and on top and sides of cake. Cover and chill thoroughly. Yield: 10 servings.

SHOPPING LIST

Staples: butter or
    margarine, hot
    sauce, lemon juice,
    mayonnaise, grated
    Parmesan cheese, salt,
    peppercorns
. . . .
1 bunch green onions
. . . .
1 (8-ounce) carton sour
    cream
2 (10-ounce) packages
    frozen green peas
. . . .
1 (6-ounce) package
    semisweet chocolate
    morsels
1 teaspoon instant coffee
    granules
2 pounds orange roughy
    fillets
1 (10.75-ounce) loaf
    pound cake
1 (2.25-ounce) package
    slivered almonds
    (for rice)
4 to 6 cups cooked rice
. . . .
Garnish: lemon and
    orange slices

Chile and Chicken Cheesecake
(page 79)

Let the Party Begin

Cranberry Christmas Punch
(page 82)

Pinwheels
(page 81)

EGGNOG DIP

Billowy peaks of this spirited dip beckon fresh fruit to take a dive. Sprinkle the dip with nutmeg if you'd like.

1½ cups refrigerated eggnog
2 tablespoons cornstarch
½ cup whipping cream

1 tablespoon sugar
½ cup sour cream
1 tablespoon light rum (optional)

Combine eggnog and cornstarch in a medium saucepan; cook over medium heat, stirring constantly, until thickened and bubbly. Remove from heat; cover with plastic wrap, gently pressing directly onto mixture. Let cool in refrigerator.

Beat whipping cream at high speed of an electric mixer until foamy; add sugar, beating until soft peaks form. Fold whipped cream, sour cream, and rum, if desired, into eggnog mixture. Cover and chill 8 hours. Serve with fresh fruit. Yield: 3 cups.

WARM ARTICHOKE DIP WITH PUMPERNICKEL BREAD

Gutsy goat cheese adds savory impact to this popular party fare. Scoop up the creamy dip with toasted pumpernickel wedges.

1 (8-ounce) carton sour cream
1 cup mayonnaise
½ cup crumbled goat cheese
¼ cup freshly grated Parmesan cheese
1 (14-ounce) can artichoke hearts, drained and coarsely chopped

Pumpernickel bread slices, cut into wedges and lightly toasted
Softened butter
Chopped fresh parsley

Combine first 5 ingredients; spoon into a lightly greased 1-quart baking dish. Bake, uncovered, at 350° for 35 minutes or until thoroughly heated.

Spread points of pumpernickel wedges with butter; sprinkle with parsley. Serve pumpernickel wedges with warm dip. Yield: 3 cups.

HOT SEAFOOD DIP

You'll find a lump of crabmeat or a shapely little shrimp in every bite. If small shrimp are unavailable, substitute medium-size, and cut them in half.

1¼ pounds unpeeled small fresh shrimp
2 tablespoons butter or margarine
2 cups mayonnaise
1 cup freshly grated Parmesan cheese
½ cup chopped green onions
3 jalapeño peppers, seeded and chopped

2 tablespoons lemon juice
2 or 3 drops of hot sauce
1 pound fresh lump crabmeat, drained
2 (14-ounce) cans artichoke hearts, drained and finely chopped
½ teaspoon salt
⅓ cup sliced almonds

Peel shrimp, and devein, if desired.

Cook shrimp in butter in a medium skillet over medium-high heat 2 minutes, stirring constantly. Drain and set aside.

Combine mayonnaise and next 5 ingredients in a large bowl. Add shrimp, crab-meat, artichoke hearts, and salt; stir well. Spoon into a greased 13- x 9- x 2-inch baking dish. Sprinkle with almonds.

Bake, uncovered, at 375° for 25 minutes or until mixture is thoroughly heated. Serve with melba toast rounds. Yield: 9 cups.

CRANBERRY-GLAZED BRIE

1 (12-ounce) package fresh
   cranberries
¾ cup firmly packed brown sugar
⅓ cup currants
⅓ cup water
⅛ teaspoon dry mustard

⅛ teaspoon ground ginger
⅛ teaspoon ground cardamom
⅛ teaspoon ground allspice
⅛ teaspoon ground cloves
1 (35.2-ounce) round Brie

Combine first 9 ingredients in a medium saucepan. Cook over medium heat, stir-ring constantly, 8 minutes or until cranberry skins pop. Set aside, and let cool.

Slice rind from top of Brie, cutting to within ½ inch of outside edges. Place Brie on a baking sheet; spoon cranberry mixture over top of Brie. Bake at 300° for 20 to 25 minutes or until cheese is softened, but not melted. Transfer to a serving platter. Serve with assorted crackers. Yield: 18 appetizer servings.

GARLIC-HERB CHEESE SPREAD

½ cup fresh parsley sprigs pinched
   from stems
1 tablespoon fresh thyme leaves
1 tablespoon fresh basil
1 tablespoon fresh tarragon
1 clove garlic
2 (8-ounce) packages cream cheese
½ cup butter or margarine, softened
1 teaspoon Worcestershire sauce

½ teaspoon red wine vinegar
3 cups (12 ounces) shredded sharp
   Cheddar cheese
⅓ cup sour cream
¼ cup butter or margarine, softened
¼ cup milk
3 tablespoons fresh sage leaves
1 tablespoon chopped fresh chives
1 teaspoon Dijon mustard

Sage leaves, chive sprigs, or violets make an easy and elegant garnish for this buttery-rich spread.

Line a 1½-quart soufflé dish with plastic wrap, leaving a 1-inch overhang around edges. Set aside.

Position knife blade in food processor bowl; add first 5 ingredients, and process until finely chopped. Add cream cheese and next 3 ingredients; process until blended. Spoon mixture into prepared dish, spreading evenly.

Combine Cheddar cheese and next 3 ingredients in processor; process until smooth, stopping once to scrape down sides. Add sage, chives, and mustard; process until combined. Spoon mixture over cream cheese layer, spreading evenly. Cover and chill at least 8 hours. Unmold onto a serving platter. Serve with crackers. Yield: 5 cups.

PECAN CHEESE BALL

2 (8-ounce) packages cream cheese,
   softened
1 (8-ounce) can crushed pineapple,
   drained
¼ cup chopped green pepper

2 tablespoons finely chopped onion
1 tablespoon seasoned salt
2 cups chopped pecans, toasted and
   divided

Combine first 5 ingredients; stir in 1 cup pecans. Cover and chill until firm.
   Shape mixture into a ball; roll in remaining 1 cup pecans. Place cheese ball on a serving platter; serve with crackers and strips of green pepper and sweet red pepper. Yield: one 5-inch cheese ball.

CHILE AND CHICKEN CHEESECAKE

2 teaspoons chicken-flavored
  bouillon granules
1 tablespoon hot water
3 (8-ounce) packages cream cheese,
  softened
1½ teaspoons chili powder
½ to 1 teaspoon hot sauce

2 large eggs
1 cup finely chopped cooked chicken
1 (4.5-ounce) can chopped green
  chiles, drained
Shredded Cheddar cheese (optional)
Sliced green onions (optional)

Dissolve bouillon granules in hot water; set aside.

Beat cream cheese at high speed of an electric mixer until creamy. Add chili powder and hot sauce; beat well. Add eggs, one at a time, beating well after each addition. Add bouillon mixture; beat well. Stir in chicken and chiles. Spoon mixture into a lightly greased 9-inch springform pan.

Bake at 300° for 45 minutes. Turn oven off, and partially open oven door; leave cheesecake in oven 1 hour. Remove cheesecake from oven, and let stand 15 minutes.

Place cheesecake on a serving platter; carefully remove sides of springform pan. If desired, top cheesecake with shredded cheese and sliced green onions. Serve cheesecake warm with tortilla chips. Yield: 16 appetizer servings.

Note: To serve cheesecake chilled, remove from oven, and let cool to room temperature on a wire rack. Cover and chill several hours. Carefully remove sides of springform pan when ready to serve.

Creamy cheesecake takes on spunky south-of-the-border flavor in this savory appetizer. Serve it with crispy tortilla chips to carry out its south-western theme. See it pictured on page 74.

BAKED GARLIC WITH SUN-DRIED TOMATOES

4 large heads garlic, unpeeled
¼ cup olive oil
2½ tablespoons butter or
  margarine, melted
2 cups dried tomatoes
2 cups chicken broth
2 teaspoons fines herbes

½ teaspoon freshly ground
  pepper
6 ounces goat cheese, sliced
Garnish: fresh basil leaves
1 (16-ounce) loaf Italian bread,
  sliced

Peel outer skins from garlic heads, keeping heads intact. Cut off top one-fourth of each head, and discard.

Place garlic heads, cut side up, in an 8-inch square baking dish; drizzle with oil and butter. Arrange tomatoes around garlic; pour broth over tomatoes. Sprinkle with fines herbes and pepper.

Bake, uncovered, at 375° for 1 hour and 15 minutes, basting tomatoes and garlic every 15 minutes with broth. Arrange cheese slices over tomatoes; bake 5 more minutes or until cheese softens. Garnish, if desired. Serve warm with bread slices. Yield: 6 appetizer servings.

Mellow roasted garlic, robust dried toma-toes, and tangy goat cheese create this Mediterranean-inspired appetizer.

ZUCCHINI STUFFED MUSHROOMS

3¼ cups shredded zucchini
¼ teaspoon salt
30 large fresh mushrooms (about 2 pounds)
¼ cup unsalted butter or margarine, melted and divided
1 clove garlic, minced

¾ cup part-skim ricotta cheese
⅓ cup crushed saltine crackers
¼ cup grated Parmesan cheese
4 oil-packed dried tomatoes, finely chopped
¼ teaspoon dried oregano
⅛ teaspoon pepper

Combine zucchini and salt in a colander; let stand 30 minutes. Press zucchini between paper towels to remove excess moisture. Set aside.

Clean mushrooms with damp paper towels. Remove stems; reserve for another use. Brush mushroom caps with 3 tablespoons butter. Place on a rack in broiler pan. Set aside.

Cook garlic in remaining 1 tablespoon butter in a large skillet over medium-high heat 1 minute, stirring constantly. Add zucchini, and cook 2 more minutes. Remove from heat, and let cool slightly. Stir in ricotta cheese and remaining 5 ingredients. Spoon mixture evenly into mushroom caps. Bake at 375° for 20 minutes. Serve immediately. Yield: 2½ dozen.

ELEGANT SHRIMP ROUNDS

If you'd like to prepare this appetizer ahead, spread the shrimp mixture on the toasted bread rounds; then cover and chill up to 8 hours before broiling.

3 cups water
1 pound unpeeled medium-size fresh shrimp
30 slices sandwich bread, toasted
1 clove garlic, minced
2 tablespoons butter or margarine, melted
1 tablespoon dry white wine
1 teaspoon grated lime rind
1 teaspoon chopped fresh dill

1 cup plus 2 tablespoons mayonnaise
1 cup grated Gruyère cheese
1 tablespoon finely chopped green onions
2 teaspoons finely chopped fresh parsley
¼ teaspoon salt
⅛ teaspoon pepper

Bring water to a boil; add shrimp, and cook 3 to 5 minutes or until shrimp turn pink. Drain well; rinse with cold water. Chill.

Peel shrimp, and devein, if desired. Finely chop shrimp; set aside.

Cut rounds from each slice of bread, using a 2½-inch biscuit cutter; set aside.

Cook garlic in butter in a large skillet over medium-high heat 30 seconds, stirring constantly. Remove from heat; stir in shrimp, wine, lime rind, and dill. Let cool. Add mayonnaise and remaining 5 ingredients; stir well. Cover and chill 1 hour.

Spread 1 heaping tablespoon shrimp mixture on each bread round. Place on ungreased baking sheets; broil 3 inches from heat (with electric oven door partially opened) 3 minutes or until golden. Serve immediately. Yield: 2½ dozen.

PINWHEELS

2 green onions, finely chopped
2 (8-ounce) packages cream cheese
1 (1-ounce) envelope Ranch-style
  dressing mix
5 (12-inch) flour tortillas
¾ cup finely chopped pimiento-
  stuffed olives

¾ cup finely chopped ripe olives
1 (4.5-ounce) can chopped green
  chiles, drained
1 (4-ounce) jar diced pimiento,
  drained

Combine first 3 ingredients; spread evenly over 1 side of tortillas.

Combine olives, chiles, and pimiento; spread over cream cheese layer. Roll up tightly, jellyroll fashion. Wrap in plastic wrap; chill at least 2 hours. To serve, remove plastic wrap, and cut each roll into 1-inch slices. Yield: 40 pinwheels.

These party pinwheels adapt to your schedule nicely. You can make them up to 24 hours in advance. Find them pictured on page 75.

BLUE CHEESE-WALNUT WAFERS

1 (4-ounce) package blue cheese,
  softened
½ cup butter, softened

1¼ cups all-purpose flour
⅛ teaspoon salt
⅓ cup finely chopped walnuts

Position knife blade in food processor; add first 4 ingredients. Process until blended, stopping once to scrape down sides. (Mixture will be sticky.) Transfer mixture to a bowl; stir in walnuts. Cover and chill 5 minutes. Divide dough in half. Shape each portion into an 8-inch log. Wrap in heavy-duty plastic wrap; chill 1 hour or until firm.

Slice dough into ¼-inch slices; place on ungreased baking sheets. Bake at 350° for 12 minutes or until lightly browned. Let cool on wire racks. Store in airtight container up to 1 week. Yield: 4½ dozen.

If you're tempted to substitute margarine for butter in this recipe, don't. The butter makes these wafers wonderfully short and the dough easier to handle.

GOUDA-CASHEW BOUCHÉES

1½ cups (6 ounces) shredded Gouda
  cheese
½ cup butter or margarine, softened
1½ cups all-purpose flour

1 teaspoon dry mustard
⅛ teaspoon salt
24 whole cashews

Combine cheese and butter in a large mixing bowl; beat at medium speed of an electric mixer until blended.

Combine flour, mustard, and salt; add to cheese mixture, beating until dough is no longer crumbly. Shape into 24 (1-inch) balls. Place on lightly greased baking sheets; gently press a cashew on top of each ball. Bake at 375° for 16 to 18 minutes or until lightly browned. Let cool on wire racks. Yield: 2 dozen.

Bouchée is French for "small patty" or "mouthful." Each one of these savory mouthfuls is crowned with a buttery cashew.

SPICED COFFEE-EGGNOG PUNCH

2 cups strongly brewed coffee
1½ (3-inch) sticks cinnamon
6 whole allspice
6 whole cloves
2 (32-ounce) cans eggnog, chilled

1 tablespoon vanilla extract
1 cup whipping cream, whipped
1 quart vanilla ice cream, softened
Ground nutmeg

Combine first 4 ingredients in a saucepan. Bring to a boil; reduce heat, and simmer, uncovered, 15 minutes. Pour coffee mixture through a wire-mesh strainer into a bowl, discarding spices; chill. Combine coffee mixture, eggnog, and vanilla in a large bowl; fold in whipped cream.

Spoon softened ice cream into a punch bowl. Pour eggnog mixture over ice cream, and stir gently. Sprinkle punch with ground nutmeg. Yield: 11 cups.

CRANBERRY CHRISTMAS PUNCH

The vibrant red color of this fizzy cranberry punch makes it perfect for a holiday gathering. Look for it on page 75.

1 (3-ounce) package cherry-flavored gelatin
1 cup boiling water
1 (6-ounce) can frozen orange juice concentrate

1 (32-ounce) bottle cranberry juice, chilled
3 cups cold water
1 (12-ounce) can ginger ale, chilled

Dissolve gelatin in boiling water. Add orange juice concentrate, stirring until it melts. Stir in cranberry juice and water. Slowly pour cherry mixture into a punch bowl. Gently stir in ginger ale. Serve immediately. Yield: 11 cups.

SHERRY WASSAIL

Come in out of the cold for a comforting mug of this traditional holiday drink—its warmth and fruity aroma are sure to cheer up frosty spirits.

2 quarts apple cider
½ cup firmly packed brown sugar
⅓ cup lemon juice
⅓ cup frozen orange juice concentrate
1½ teaspoons ground nutmeg
6 (3-inch) sticks cinnamon

3 whole cloves
3 whole allspice
2 (750-milliliter) bottles dry sherry
Garnish: orange slices studded with whole cloves

Combine first 8 ingredients in a Dutch oven. Bring to a boil; cover, reduce heat, and simmer 20 minutes. Discard whole spices. Stir in sherry; heat just until mixture begins to simmer, stirring occasionally. If desired, transfer mixture to a heat-proof punch bowl; garnish, if desired. Serve warm. Yield: 15 cups.

WHITE CHOCOLATE BRANDY ALEXANDER

3½ cups milk
½ teaspoon vanilla extract
⅛ teaspoon salt
6 ounces white chocolate, finely
  chopped

⅓ cup brandy
3 tablespoons white crème de cacao
Garnishes: whipped cream, white
  chocolate shavings

Combine first 3 ingredients in a medium saucepan; cook over medium heat until thoroughly heated (do not boil). Remove from heat; gradually stir about one-fourth of hot mixture into chocolate, stirring with a wire whisk until chocolate melts. Add to remaining hot mixture, stirring constantly. Stir in brandy and crème de cacao. Pour into glasses. Garnish, if desired. Serve immediately. Yield: 4½ cups.

Entrées for Every Occasion

Happy Holiday Hens
(page 92)

STUFFED SOLE WITH NUTMEG SAUCE

A simple green vegetable will complete the meal nicely.

2 tablespoons butter, divided
1 green onion, chopped
⅓ cup shredded carrot
½ cup cooked rice
1 teaspoon grated lemon rind, divided
1 teaspoon fresh lemon juice, divided
½ teaspoon ground nutmeg, divided

½ teaspoon salt
¼ teaspoon pepper
4 small sole fillets (about 10 ounces total)
1 tablespoon plus 1 teaspoon all-purpose flour
¾ cup canned low-sodium chicken broth, undiluted
¼ cup dry white wine
1 tablespoon chopped fresh parsley

Melt 1 tablespoon butter in a heavy skillet over medium heat; cook onion and carrot in butter 3 to 5 minutes or until tender, stirring occasionally. Stir in rice, ½ teaspoon lemon rind, ½ teaspoon lemon juice, ¼ teaspoon nutmeg, salt, and pepper.

Spoon one-fourth of rice mixture onto end of each fillet; roll up fillets, and place, seam side down, in a lightly greased 11- x 7- x 1½-inch baking dish. Bake at 350° for 20 minutes or until fish flakes easily when tested with a fork. Keep warm.

Melt remaining 1 tablespoon butter in a heavy saucepan over low heat; add flour, stirring until smooth. Cook 1 minute, stirring constantly. Gradually add chicken broth; cook over medium heat, stirring constantly, until mixture is thickened and bubbly. Stir in remaining ½ teaspoon lemon rind, ½ teaspoon lemon juice, and ¼ teaspoon nutmeg. Stir in wine and parsley; cook until thoroughly heated. Serve over fillets. Yield: 2 servings.

BAKED SALMON WITH WINE

Sweeter than most white wines, Sauterne accentuates the earthy hickory-smoked salt in this salmon. Find the smoked salt in the spice section of your supermarket.

5 (6-ounce) salmon fillets
¾ cup Sauterne or other sweet white wine
¼ cup vegetable oil
3 large cloves garlic, minced

2 tablespoons soy sauce
1 teaspoon salt
Vegetable cooking spray
¾ teaspoon hickory-smoked salt, divided

Place fillets in a large heavy-duty, zip-top plastic bag. Combine wine and next 4 ingredients in container of an electric blender; process 30 seconds. Pour ¾ cup marinade over fillets. Seal bag securely; marinate in refrigerator 3 hours, turning occasionally. Chill remaining marinade for basting.

Remove fillets from marinade, discarding marinade. Place fillets in a 13- x 9- x 2-inch baking dish coated with cooking spray; sprinkle with ¼ teaspoon hickory-smoked salt. Bake at 350° for 15 minutes or until fish flakes easily when tested with a fork, basting twice with reserved marinade and sprinkling with remaining ½ teaspoon hickory-smoked salt. Yield: 5 servings.

HERBED STEAK WITH RED PEPPER-SAFFRON CREAM SAUCE

1 teaspoon kosher salt
4 (8-ounce) rib-eye steaks (1 inch thick)
2½ teaspoons coarsely ground pepper
2 teaspoons chopped fresh thyme
1 teaspoon chopped fresh rosemary

3 cloves garlic, minced, or ½ teaspoon garlic powder
1½ tablespoons extra-light olive oil
Red Pepper-Saffron Cream Sauce
Garnish: fresh rosemary or thyme sprigs

Sprinkle salt on both sides of steaks; let stand 10 minutes. Combine pepper and next 3 ingredients; rub mixture on both sides of steaks.

Heat olive oil in a large skillet over medium-high heat. Add steaks; reduce heat, and cook 4 minutes on each side or to desired degree of doneness. Serve with Red Pepper-Saffron Cream Sauce. Garnish, if desired. Yield: 4 servings.

RED PEPPER-SAFFRON CREAM SAUCE

1 (7-ounce) jar diced pimiento, drained
⅔ cup beef broth

½ cup whipping cream
½ teaspoon threads of saffron
2 teaspoons lemon juice

Combine first 4 ingredients in a saucepan. Bring to a boil; reduce heat, and simmer, uncovered, until mixture is reduced by half. Cool slightly. Pour mixture into container of an electric blender. Add juice; process until smooth. Yield: ¾ cup.

Saffron colors the delicate cream sauce burnt orange. The full-bodied sauce is ready when it's reduced by half. Measure its depth before and during cooking by standing a wooden spoon on its handle end in the saucepan.

MARINATED BEEF ROAST

1 (3½-pound) eye-of-round roast
⅓ cup soy sauce
⅓ cup lime juice
⅓ cup sherry
¼ cup chopped fresh cilantro

3 tablespoons minced garlic
2 tablespoons vegetable oil
1 tablespoon minced fresh ginger
1 tablespoon maple syrup

Place roast in a large heavy-duty, zip-top plastic bag. Combine soy sauce and remaining 7 ingredients. Pour over roast. Seal bag; marinate in refrigerator 8 to 12 hours, turning occasionally.

Remove roast from marinade, reserving marinade. Bring marinade to a boil, and set aside.

Place roast on a rack in a roasting pan. Bake roast, uncovered, at 350° for 1½ hours or until meat thermometer inserted in thickest part of roast registers 145° (medium-rare) or 160° (medium), basting every 30 minutes with reserved marinade. Yield: 10 servings.

This may be the most tender eye-of-round roast we've ever tasted. The succulent meat is full of flavor with its marinade of soy sauce, lime juice, and sherry.

BEEF AND THREE-CHEESE TETRAZZINI

Cream cheese and cottage cheese in the pasta provide a velvety contrast to the meaty sauce in this make-ahead dinner. Parmesan atop the pasta casserole completes the cheesy trio.

1½ pounds ground chuck
½ cup chopped onion
1 teaspoon salt
¼ teaspoon pepper
1 (15-ounce) can tomato sauce
8 ounces linguine or spaghetti, uncooked

1 (8-ounce) package cream cheese
1 cup cottage cheese
¼ cup sour cream
¼ cup chopped green pepper
¼ cup sliced green onions
¼ cup freshly grated Parmesan cheese

Cook ground chuck and chopped onion in a large skillet over medium-high heat, stirring constantly, until meat crumbles. Drain.

Return meat and onion to skillet; add salt, pepper, and tomato sauce. Cook 10 minutes over medium-low heat, stirring occasionally.

Cook linguine according to package directions. Drain and set aside.

Combine cream cheese, cottage cheese, and sour cream; stir well. Stir in green pepper and green onions. Add linguine; stir well. Spoon linguine mixture into a greased 13- x 9- x 2-inch baking dish. Pour meat sauce over top. Sprinkle with Parmesan cheese. Bake at 325° for 30 minutes. Yield: 8 servings.

Sautéed Veal Scallops with Marsala Sauce

1 cup all-purpose flour
1 teaspoon salt
½ teaspoon pepper
1½ pounds veal cutlets
¼ cup butter or margarine, melted and divided

3 tablespoons olive oil, divided
½ cup dry Marsala
½ cup beef broth, divided

Mashed potatoes on the side complement the veal and soak up the Marsala sauce at the same time.

Combine flour, salt, and pepper. Dredge veal in flour mixture. Brown half of veal in 1 tablespoon melted butter and 1½ tablespoons oil in a large skillet over medium-high heat. Transfer veal to a serving platter. Repeat procedure with remaining veal, adding 1 tablespoon melted butter and 1½ tablespoons oil.

Add Marsala and ¼ cup broth to skillet. Bring to a boil over high heat; cook 1 minute, stirring constantly. Return veal to skillet; cover, reduce heat, and simmer 10 minutes. Transfer veal to a platter.

Add remaining ¼ cup broth to skillet; cook 1 minute, stirring constantly. Remove from heat; stir in remaining 2 tablespoons butter. Drizzle Marsala sauce over veal. Yield: 4 to 6 servings.

Pork with Red Plum Sauce

1 (4-pound) rolled boneless pork loin roast
¼ teaspoon onion salt
¼ teaspoon garlic salt
1 cup water
¾ cup chopped onion
2 tablespoons butter or margarine, melted

1 (10-ounce) jar red plum preserves
½ cup firmly packed brown sugar
⅓ cup chili sauce
¼ cup soy sauce
2 tablespoons lemon juice
2 teaspoons prepared mustard
3 drops of hot sauce

Irresistibly tender and heightened with a lavish plum sauce, this pork roast received our best rating. Pair it with risotto and steamed broccoli for a company-worthy entrée as pictured on page 2.

Remove strings from roast; trim fat. Sprinkle roast with onion salt and garlic salt. Reroll roast, tying securely at 2-inch intervals with heavy string. Place roast on a rack in a roasting pan; add water to pan. Cover with aluminum foil, and bake at 325° for 2 hours. Drain and discard drippings.

Cook onion in butter in a medium saucepan over medium-high heat, stirring constantly, until tender. Add preserves and remaining 6 ingredients. Cook over medium heat, uncovered, 15 minutes, stirring often.

Pour half of sauce over roast. Bake, uncovered, 20 more minutes or until meat thermometer inserted in thickest part of roast registers 160° (medium), basting with half of remaining sauce. Transfer roast to a serving platter; let stand 10 minutes before serving. Serve remaining sauce with roast. Yield: 12 servings.

GOURMET VENISON ROAST

Mash cooked potatoes, peel and all, to make a fitting companion for this rustic roast.

1 (5-pound) venison chuck roast, trimmed
2 cups water
1 cup white vinegar
3 cloves garlic, finely chopped
2 stalks celery with leaves, finely chopped
1 large onion, finely chopped
1 medium-size green pepper, finely chopped
2 tablespoons vegetable oil
½ cup plus 3 tablespoons dry red wine, divided
1 tablespoon salt

1 tablespoon black pepper
1 teaspoon meat tenderizer (optional)
½ teaspoon garlic powder
¼ teaspoon ground red pepper
2 lemons, sliced
8 slices bacon
½ cup butter or margarine
½ cup fresh orange juice
½ cup honey
½ teaspoon dried rosemary
2 tablespoons cornstarch
2 tablespoons water
2 tablespoons chopped fresh parsley
4 green onions, thinly sliced

Place roast in a large heavy-duty, zip-top plastic bag. Add 2 cups water and vinegar to roast. Seal bag securely; marinate in refrigerator 8 hours, turning occasionally. Remove roast from marinade, discarding marinade. Pat roast dry with paper towels; set roast aside.

Cook chopped garlic and next 3 ingredients in hot oil in a large roasting pan, stirring constantly, 5 minutes or until tender. Place roast in pan; pour ½ cup wine over roast.

Combine salt and next 4 ingredients; sprinkle over roast. Arrange lemon slices over roast; top with bacon.

Combine remaining 3 tablespoons wine, butter, and next 3 ingredients in a small saucepan; cook over medium heat until butter melts, stirring occasionally. Baste roast once with butter mixture.

Cover and bake at 275° for 4 hours, brushing often with remaining butter mixture. Insert meat thermometer into thickest portion of roast, making sure it does not touch bone or fat. Bake, uncovered, 1 more hour or until meat thermometer registers 170°. Remove roast to a serving platter, reserving drippings in pan.

Combine cornstarch and 2 tablespoons water; gradually add to pan drippings. Bring sauce to a boil over medium-high heat, stirring constantly; cook, stirring constantly, until thickened and bubbly. Stir in parsley and green onions. Serve sauce with roast. Yield: 8 servings.

WHITE BEAN CHILI

1 pound dried Great Northern beans
2 medium onions, chopped
4 cloves garlic, minced
1 tablespoon olive oil
2 (4.5-ounce) cans chopped green
   chiles, undrained
2 teaspoons ground cumin
1½ teaspoons dried oregano
Dash of ground red pepper

6 cups chicken broth
5 cups chopped cooked chicken
   breast
3 cups (12 ounces) shredded
   Monterey Jack cheese, divided
Salt and pepper to taste
Salsa
Sour cream
Garnish: chopped fresh parsley

In a hurry?
To quick-soak dried beans, cover beans with water 2 inches above beans in a large Dutch oven. Bring to a boil; cover and cook 2 minutes. Remove from heat, and let stand 1 hour. Drain.

Sort and wash beans; place in a large Dutch oven. Cover with water 2 inches above beans; let soak 8 hours. Drain and set beans aside.

Cook onion and garlic in oil in Dutch oven over medium-high heat, stirring constantly, until tender. Add green chiles and next 3 ingredients; cook 2 minutes, stirring constantly. Add beans and chicken broth. Bring to a boil; cover, reduce heat, and simmer 2 hours or until beans are tender, stirring occasionally. Add chicken, 1 cup cheese, and salt and pepper to taste. Bring to a boil; reduce heat, and simmer, uncovered, 10 minutes, stirring often.

To serve, ladle chili into individual soup bowls. Top each serving evenly with remaining 2 cups cheese, salsa, and sour cream. Garnish, if desired. Yield: 13 cups.

CHICKEN IN CRANBERRY CREAM SAUCE

Tart dried cranberries add a burst of flavor to the buttery cream sauce. Just toss a little linguine with butter to accompany this saucy dish. Steamed fresh asparagus will add color to the plate and round out the meal.

½ cup dried cranberries
3 tablespoons Cognac
2 tablespoons Grand Marnier or other orange-flavored liqueur
4 skinned and boned chicken breast halves
½ cup all-purpose flour

2 tablespoons olive oil
2 tablespoons butter, melted
⅔ cup raspberry vinegar
2 shallots, minced
1½ cups chicken broth
1½ cups whipping cream
Garnish: fresh parsley sprigs

Combine first 3 ingredients in a small bowl; cover and let stand 30 minutes.

Dredge chicken in flour. Cook chicken in oil and butter in a large skillet over medium-high heat 5 minutes on each side or until done. Transfer chicken to a serving platter, reserving drippings in skillet. Set chicken aside, and keep warm.

Add raspberry vinegar to drippings in skillet, deglazing skillet by scraping particles that cling to bottom. Add cranberry mixture and shallots; bring to a boil. Reduce heat, and simmer, uncovered, 5 minutes. Add broth; bring to a boil. Reduce heat, and simmer, uncovered, 12 minutes. Gradually add whipping cream; cook over medium heat, stirring constantly, 6 minutes or until mixture is thickened and bubbly. Spoon sauce over chicken. Garnish, if desired. Serve immediately. Yield: 4 servings.

HAPPY HOLIDAY HENS

These hens are stuffed with rice, pecans, and apricots and coated with a glaze of apricot preserves. Find them in the photograph on page 84.

4 (1½-pound) Cornish hens
½ cup apricot preserves
⅓ cup soy sauce
½ teaspoon ground nutmeg
2 cups cooked rice
1 tablespoon plus 1 teaspoon soy sauce

½ cup minced green onions
½ cup pecan pieces, toasted
⅓ cup chopped dried apricot halves
Garnishes: fresh rosemary sprigs, whole pecans, dried apricot halves, green grapes

Remove giblets, and rinse hens thoroughly with cold water; pat dry. Lift wingtips up and over back of hens, tucking wingtips under hens.

Combine preserves, ⅓ cup soy sauce, and nutmeg. Brush cavities of hens lightly with preserve mixture.

Combine rice and 1 tablespoon plus 1 teaspoon soy sauce, stirring well. Add green onions, pecans, and apricot; stir well. Stuff hens evenly with rice mixture, and close cavities. Secure with wooden picks, and tie leg ends together with string.

Place hens, breast side up, on a lightly greased rack in a shallow roasting pan. Brush lightly with preserve mixture. Bake, uncovered, at 375° for 45 minutes. Cover and bake 45 more minutes or until done, basting with remaining preserve mixture. Garnish, if desired. Yield: 4 servings.

TRADITIONAL CHRISTMAS GOOSE WITH SWEET BREAD DRESSING

1 (10-pound) dressed goose
8 cups cubed day-old bread
3 cups chopped cooking apple
2 cups raisins
⅓ cup sugar
1 tablespoon ground cinnamon

1 teaspoon salt
¼ teaspoon ground ginger
¼ teaspoon ground mace
¼ teaspoon dried thyme
½ cup water
¼ cup butter, melted

Remove giblets and neck from goose; reserve for another use. Rinse goose thoroughly with cold water; pat dry. Prick skin with a fork at 2-inch intervals. Set goose aside.

Combine bread cubes and next 8 ingredients; stir in water and butter. Spoon bread cube mixture into cavity of goose; close cavity with skewers, and truss. Place goose, breast side up, on a rack in a shallow roasting pan. Insert meat thermometer into meaty portion of thigh, making sure it does not touch bone. Bake, uncovered, at 350° for 2½ to 3 hours or until meat thermometer registers 180° in thigh and 165° in center of stuffing.

Transfer goose to a serving platter; let stand 10 minutes before slicing. Yield: 6 to 8 servings.

Fruit and spices sweeten this bread dressing for the holidays. This recipe makes a hefty amount, so after you stuff the goose, spoon the rest of the dressing into a greased baking dish, and bake at 350° until lightly browned.

HEARTY TURKEY STEW

1¼ pounds turkey tenderloins, cubed
8 small red potatoes, unpeeled and quartered
4 medium carrots, scraped and cut into ½-inch slices
1 large onion, chopped
4 cloves garlic, minced
3 tablespoons olive oil

2 tablespoons all-purpose flour
1 (10½-ounce) can chicken broth, undiluted
1 cup dry red wine
1 teaspoon dried thyme
1 teaspoon pepper
½ pound fresh mushrooms
½ cup chopped fresh parsley

Cook first 5 ingredients in oil in a large ovenproof Dutch oven over medium-high heat 10 minutes, stirring often. Reduce heat to low. Add flour, stirring well. Cook 1 minute, stirring constantly. Add chicken broth, wine, thyme, and pepper. Bring to a boil; add mushrooms.

Place pan in oven; bake, uncovered, at 350° for 45 to 50 minutes or until turkey and vegetables are tender, stirring occasionally. Stir in parsley. Yield: 7 cups.

Carrots, potatoes, and onions fortify this hearty stew. A crusty French bread is all you really need on the side.

Acorn Squash with Pear Stuffing
(page 102)

Rounding Out the Meal

Cranberry Gorgonzola Green Salad
(page 99)

PECAN WILD RICE

Looking for a traditional menu partner for poultry? This Test-Kitchens favorite is sure to satisfy.

5½ cups chicken broth
1 cup wild rice, uncooked
4 green onions, thinly sliced
1 cup pecan halves, toasted
1 cup golden raisins
⅓ cup orange juice

¼ cup chopped fresh parsley
¼ cup olive oil
1 tablespoon grated orange rind
1½ teaspoons salt
¼ teaspoon freshly ground pepper

Combine broth and rice in a medium saucepan. Bring to a boil; reduce heat, and simmer, uncovered, 45 minutes or until rice is done. Drain and place in a medium bowl. Add green onions and remaining ingredients; toss gently. Serve immediately. Yield: 6 servings.

WILD MUSHROOM AND ONION RISOTTO

Serve this creamy Italian-inspired rice dish as an accompaniment with roast turkey or pork. It's a welcome change of pace from dressing. See it on page 2.

2½ cups chicken broth
1 cup chopped onion
1 clove garlic, crushed
2 teaspoons olive oil
1 cup Arborio or other short-grain rice, uncooked

1 (3.5-ounce) package fresh shiitake mushrooms, sliced
1 cup sliced fresh crimini mushrooms
¼ cup freshly grated Parmesan cheese
2 tablespoons dry white wine

Bring broth to a boil in a saucepan. Cover, reduce heat to low, and keep warm.

Cook onion and garlic in oil in a large skillet over medium heat, stirring constantly, until onion is tender. Add rice, and cook 4 minutes, stirring constantly. Add mushrooms and ½ cup warm broth; cook, stirring constantly, until most of the liquid is absorbed.

Continue adding warm broth, ½ cup at a time, stirring constantly, until rice is tender and mixture is creamy, allowing rice to absorb most of liquid each time before adding more broth. (The entire process should take about 25 minutes.) Stir in cheese and wine. Transfer mixture to a serving bowl; serve immediately. Yield: 6 servings.

Angel Hair Pasta with Creamy Mushroom Sauce and Fresh Herbs

2 medium shallots, minced
1 tablespoon butter or margarine, melted
1¾ cups whipping cream
½ teaspoon salt
½ teaspoon freshly ground pepper

½ pound fresh mushrooms, sliced
8 ounces angel hair pasta, uncooked
3 tablespoons minced fresh parsley, divided
3 tablespoons minced fresh chives
2 tablespoons minced fresh tarragon

Whether you serve this rich dish as an accompaniment or as a meatless entrée, you'll love the way the creamy mushroom-herb sauce bathes the delicate strands of angel hair pasta.

Cook shallots in butter in a large skillet over low heat 1 minute, stirring constantly. Add whipping cream and next 3 ingredients; bring to a boil, stirring often. Reduce heat, and simmer, uncovered, 30 minutes or until mushrooms are very tender, stirring often.

While mushrooms simmer, cook pasta according to package directions; drain. Remove mushroom mixture from heat; stir in 2 tablespoons parsley, chives, and tarragon. Pour mixture over pasta; toss. Sprinkle with remaining 1 tablespoon parsley. Serve immediately. Yield: 6 side-dish servings or 3 main-dish servings.

Fettuccine with Pistachio Sauce

1 (16-ounce) package fettuccine
¾ pound roasted and salted pistachio nuts, shelled and coarsely chopped
2 cloves garlic, pressed

¼ cup olive oil
¾ cup whipping cream
¼ teaspoon salt
¼ teaspoon pepper

Cook fettuccine according to package directions. Drain well; place in a large bowl, and keep warm.

Cook pistachio nuts and garlic in oil in a large skillet over medium-high heat, stirring constantly, 3 minutes or until nuts are toasted. Add whipping cream, salt, and pepper. Cook 2 minutes, stirring constantly. Pour pistachio sauce over fettuccine; toss until fettuccine is coated. Yield: 8 servings.

Orange-Date Salad with Peanut Butter Dressing

½ cup sour cream
½ cup creamy peanut butter
⅓ cup milk
¼ teaspoon salt
Dash of garlic powder
6 cups mixed salad greens
1 (8-ounce) package pitted dates, chopped

6 oranges, peeled, sectioned, and coarsely chopped
¼ cup chopped unsalted dry roasted peanuts
½ cup flaked coconut, toasted

Combine first 5 ingredients in a bowl; stir well with a wire whisk. Cover and chill. Place greens in a bowl. Combine dates, oranges, and peanuts; spoon over greens. Drizzle with ¼ cup dressing. Sprinkle with coconut. Serve with remaining dressing. Yield: 6 servings.

CRANBERRY GORGONZOLA GREEN SALAD

⅓ cup vegetable oil
¼ cup seasoned rice vinegar
¾ teaspoon Dijon mustard
1 clove garlic, pressed
1 small head Bibb lettuce, torn
1 small head green leaf lettuce, torn

1 Granny Smith or pippin apple, diced
⅓ cup coarsely chopped walnuts, toasted
⅓ cup dried cranberries
⅓ cup crumbled Gorgonzola cheese

Combine first 4 ingredients; stir with a wire whisk until blended. Set aside.

Just before serving, combine Bibb lettuce and remaining 5 ingredients in a large bowl. Pour dressing over salad; toss gently. Yield: 8 servings.

Tart dried cranberries and Gorgonzola contribute mighty flavor to this salad that received our highest rating. See it on page 95.

FROZEN FRUIT SALADS

¾ cup plus 2 tablespoons sugar
½ cup sifted cake flour
¼ teaspoon salt
1 cup pineapple juice
3 tablespoons lemon juice
1 large egg, lightly beaten
1 cup whipping cream
1 (16½-ounce) can white cherries in extra-heavy syrup, drained

1 (16-ounce) can sliced peaches in heavy syrup, drained
1 (8-ounce) can pineapple chunks, drained
1 medium banana, sliced
½ cup chopped pecans
¼ cup maraschino cherries, chopped
8 (8-ounce) paper drinking cups
Green leaf lettuce (optional)

Served in individual cups, this frozen fruit salad with cherries, bananas, and pecans is a great make-ahead salad for any luncheon.

Combine first 3 ingredients in top of a double boiler; stir in pineapple juice and lemon juice. Bring water in bottom of double boiler to a boil. Reduce heat to low; cook, stirring constantly, 12 minutes or until thickened. Gradually stir a small amount of hot mixture into beaten egg; add to remaining hot mixture, stirring constantly. Cook over medium heat, stirring constantly, until candy thermometer registers 160° and mixture thickens (about 3 minutes). Remove from heat; let cool slightly. Cover and chill thoroughly.

Beat whipping cream at medium speed of an electric mixer until stiff peaks form. Fold whipped cream into chilled mixture. Stir in white cherries and next 5 ingredients. Spoon mixture evenly into paper cup-lined muffin pans. Cover and freeze at least 8 hours.

To serve, peel paper cup away from each salad. Serve on lettuce leaves, if desired. Yield: 8 servings.

BROCCOLI IN OLIVE-NUT SAUCE

3 pounds fresh broccoli
1 teaspoon lemon-pepper seasoning
¼ cup sliced ripe olives
2 cloves garlic, crushed

3 tablespoons lemon juice
½ cup butter or margarine, melted
½ cup slivered almonds, toasted

Remove and discard broccoli leaves and tough ends of stalks; cut into flowerets. Arrange broccoli in a steamer basket over boiling water. Cover and steam 5 minutes or until crisp-tender. Arrange broccoli on a serving platter; sprinkle with lemon-pepper seasoning. Set aside, and keep warm.

Cook olives, garlic, and lemon juice in butter in a small skillet over medium-high heat 3 minutes, stirring constantly. Stir in almonds. Spoon sauce over broccoli. Serve immediately. Yield: 8 servings.

BACON-PECAN BRUSSELS SPROUTS

Shredded brussels sprouts burst with flavor when paired with crisp bacon and toasted pecans.

1 pound fresh brussels sprouts
5 slices bacon
¼ cup chopped pecans
2 green onions, sliced

⅛ teaspoon ground nutmeg
⅛ teaspoon salt
⅛ teaspoon pepper

Wash brussels sprouts thoroughly; remove discolored leaves. Cut off stem ends; cut brussels sprouts vertically into thin shreds. Set aside.

Cook bacon in a skillet until crisp. Remove bacon, reserving drippings in skillet. Crumble bacon; set aside. Add pecans to drippings; cook over medium-high heat, stirring constantly, until golden. Add brussels sprouts, green onions, nutmeg, salt, and pepper. Cook over medium heat 18 minutes or until brussels sprouts are tender, stirring often. Spoon into a serving dish; sprinkle with bacon. Yield: 4 servings.

GLAZED CARROTS

These baby carrots glisten with a glaze of brown sugar, honey, orange juice, and lemon juice.

2 (10-ounce) packages frozen baby
  carrots
½ cup butter or margarine, melted
2 tablespoons brown sugar

1 tablespoon grated orange rind
2 tablespoons fresh orange juice
1 tablespoon honey
2 teaspoons lemon juice

Cook baby carrots according to package directions until crisp-tender; drain well.

Place carrots in an ungreased 1½-quart baking dish. Drizzle melted butter evenly over carrots. Sprinkle brown sugar evenly over carrots.

Combine orange rind, fresh orange juice, honey, and lemon juice, stirring well. Drizzle orange juice mixture over carrot mixture. Bake, uncovered, at 325° for 30 minutes, stirring and basting often. Yield: 6 servings.

LEMON-ROSEMARY GREEN BEANS

2 pounds small fresh green beans
3 tablespoons butter
1 tablespoon minced fresh rosemary
½ teaspoon grated lemon rind
½ teaspoon salt
¼ teaspoon freshly ground pepper
Garnish: lemon curl

Wash beans; trim ends, and remove strings. Cook beans in boiling water to cover 8 minutes or until crisp-tender; drain. Plunge into ice water briefly to stop the cooking process; drain again. Pat beans dry with paper towels. Transfer beans to a bowl.

Combine butter and next 4 ingredients in a small saucepan; cook over low heat until butter melts, stirring mixture occasionally. Pour butter mixture over beans, and toss gently. Garnish, if desired. Yield: 6 servings.

GRATIN OF CAULIFLOWER

Buttery breadcrumbs with a hint of ginger blanket this cheesy cauli-flower casserole.

1 (1½-pound) cauliflower, broken into flowerets
3 tablespoons butter or margarine, divided
2 tablespoons all-purpose flour
¼ teaspoon salt
¼ teaspoon ground nutmeg
1 cup half-and-half

¼ cup (1 ounce) shredded Swiss cheese
1 teaspoon lemon juice
3 drops of hot sauce
¼ cup soft breadcrumbs
⅛ teaspoon ground ginger
2 tablespoons freshly grated Parmesan cheese

Cook cauliflower in a small amount of boiling water 10 minutes or until tender; drain. Place cauliflower in a lightly greased 11- x 7- x 1½-inch baking dish.

Melt 2 tablespoons butter in a medium saucepan over low heat; add flour, salt, and nutmeg, stirring until smooth. Cook 1 minute, stirring constantly. Gradually add half-and-half; cook over medium heat, stirring constantly, until mixture is thickened and bubbly. Stir in Swiss cheese, lemon juice, and hot sauce. Pour sauce mixture over cauliflower, and set aside.

Melt remaining 1 tablespoon butter in a small skillet over medium heat; stir in breadcrumbs and ginger. Cook, stirring constantly, until golden. Spoon crumb mixture over cauliflower; sprinkle with Parmesan cheese. Bake, uncovered, at 350° for 20 minutes. Let stand 5 minutes before serving. Yield: 4 to 6 servings.

PEAS PERNOD

A spritz of licorice-essence Pernod coaxes out the sassy horse-radish and mint flavors in this chilled English pea side dish.

1 (8-ounce) carton sour cream
1 tablespoon chopped fresh mint
1 teaspoon prepared horseradish
½ teaspoon salt
½ teaspoon Pernod or anisette

2 (10-ounce) packages frozen English peas, thawed
3 green onions, chopped
1 Red Delicious apple, cored and chopped

Combine first 5 ingredients in a large bowl, stirring well. Pat peas dry on paper towels to remove excess moisture; add peas to sour cream mixture. Add green onions and apple; toss gently. Cover and chill thoroughly. Yield: 6 servings.

ACORN SQUASH WITH PEAR STUFFING

See this elegant holiday accompaniment on page 94.

2 acorn squash
1 small onion, chopped (¾ cup)
¼ cup butter or margarine, melted
2 tablespoons brown sugar
2 tablespoons bourbon

½ teaspoon ground ginger
½ teaspoon ground nutmeg
¼ teaspoon ground mace
2 medium pears, peeled, cored, and chopped

Cut each squash in half lengthwise; remove and discard seeds and membranes. Place squash halves, cut side down, in a 13- x 9- x 2-inch baking dish. Add water to dish to depth of 1 inch. Cover and bake at 400° for 45 minutes. Drain. Return squash halves to dish, cut side up. Set aside.

Cook onion in butter in a large skillet over medium-high heat, stirring constantly, until tender. Stir in brown sugar and next 4 ingredients. Add pear; cook 5 minutes, stirring occasionally. Spoon pear mixture evenly into squash cavities. Bake at 350° for 15 minutes. Yield: 4 servings.

SQUASH CASSEROLE

1 pound yellow squash, sliced
1 medium onion, chopped
⅓ cup water
¼ teaspoon salt
¾ cup (3 ounces) shredded Cheddar cheese, divided
½ cup fine, dry breadcrumbs or buttery cracker crumbs, divided

¼ cup butter or margarine
2 large eggs, lightly beaten
1 tablespoon sugar
¼ teaspoon salt
¼ teaspoon soy sauce
⅛ teaspoon pepper
⅛ teaspoon paprika

Combine squash, onion, water, and ¼ teaspoon salt in a saucepan. Bring to a boil; reduce heat, and simmer, uncovered, 15 minutes or until vegetables are tender. Drain and mash squash mixture. Add ½ cup cheese, ¼ cup breadcrumbs, butter, and next 5 ingredients; stir well. Spoon into a lightly greased 1½-quart casserole.

Bake, uncovered, at 350° for 20 minutes; top with remaining ¼ cup cheese and remaining ¼ cup breadcrumbs. Sprinkle with paprika, and bake 15 more minutes or until cheese melts and mixture is thoroughly heated. Yield: 4 servings.

PRALINE SWEET POTATO CASSEROLE

4 cups mashed cooked sweet potato (about 4½ pounds)
½ cup firmly packed brown sugar
⅓ cup half-and-half
3 tablespoons butter, melted
2 teaspoons brandy extract
1 teaspoon salt
1 teaspoon grated orange peel

½ teaspoon ground ginger
½ teaspoon ground cinnamon
¼ teaspoon ground allspice
⅛ teaspoon pepper
⅓ cup firmly packed brown sugar
½ cup chopped pecans
¼ cup butter, melted
½ teaspoon ground cinnamon

Crowned with a brown sugar and pecan topping, this sweet potato dish is destined to become a holiday favorite.

Combine first 11 ingredients; spoon into a lightly greased 11- x 7- x 1½-inch baking dish.

Combine ⅓ cup brown sugar and remaining 3 ingredients; sprinkle over potato mixture. Bake at 350° for 30 minutes or until thoroughly heated. Yield: 8 servings.

Sour Cream Cinnamon
Buns (page 112)

Bread Shoppe

Cranberry-Pumpkin Bread
(page 107)

SWEET POTATO BISCUITS

⅓ cup butter or margarine
2½ cups biscuit mix

1 cup canned mashed sweet potato
½ cup milk

Cut butter into biscuit mix with a pastry blender until mixture is crumbly. Combine sweet potato and milk; add to biscuit mix mixture, stirring with a fork just until dry ingredients are moistened.

Turn dough out onto a lightly floured surface; knead 4 or 5 times. Roll to ½-inch thickness; cut with a 2-inch biscuit cutter. Place biscuits on a large ungreased baking sheet. Bake at 450° for 10 to 12 minutes or until golden. Yield: 22 biscuits.

PECAN POPOVERS

These puffy popovers are light and airy on the inside and crispy on the outside.

¼ cup plus 2 tablespoons butter, softened
¼ cup plus 2 tablespoons honey
¾ teaspoon grated lemon rind
1 cup all-purpose flour

½ teaspoon salt
1 cup milk
2 large eggs, lightly beaten
¼ cup finely chopped pecans

Combine first 3 ingredients; stir well, and chill. Combine flour and next 3 ingredients; beat with a wire whisk just until smooth. Stir in pecans. Pour batter evenly into six 6-ounce greased custard cups. Bake at 425° for 30 minutes or until golden. Serve immediately with chilled butter mixture. Yield: 6 popovers.

FRESH LEMON-GLAZED MUFFINS

To make the lemons easier to juice, roll them on a flat surface, pressing firmly with the palm of your hand.

1¾ cups all-purpose flour
1½ teaspoons baking powder
½ teaspoon baking soda
¼ teaspoon salt
½ cup sugar
2 teaspoons grated lemon rind

2 large eggs, lightly beaten
⅔ cup fresh lemon juice
½ cup unsalted butter, melted
1 teaspoon lemon extract
¼ cup sugar
¼ cup fresh lemon juice

Combine first 6 ingredients in a large bowl; make a well in center of mixture.

Combine eggs and next 3 ingredients; add to flour mixture, stirring just until dry ingredients are moistened. Spoon batter into eight paper-lined muffin pans. Bake at 400° for 20 to 25 minutes or until a wooden pick inserted in center comes out clean.

Combine ¼ cup sugar and ¼ cup lemon juice in a small saucepan; cook over medium heat, stirring constantly, until sugar dissolves.

Remove muffins from oven, and poke holes in tops of muffins with a wooden pick; drizzle with warm glaze. Cool muffins in pans 5 minutes; remove from pans, and let cool completely on a wire rack. Yield: 8 muffins.

MACADAMIA NUT-BANANA BREAD

2¼ cups all-purpose flour
1 tablespoon plus ½ teaspoon baking
  powder
½ teaspoon salt
¾ cup firmly packed brown sugar
¼ cup sugar
1½ teaspoons ground cinnamon

1¼ cups mashed ripe banana
⅓ cup milk
3 tablespoons vegetable oil
1 large egg
1 teaspoon white vinegar
1 cup macadamia nuts, coarsely
  chopped

Combine first 6 ingredients in a large bowl; make a well in center of mixture.
   Combine banana, milk, oil, egg, and vinegar; beat with a wire whisk until blended. Add to dry ingredients, stirring just until moistened. Stir in macadamia nuts.
   Spoon batter into a greased 9- x 5- x 3-inch loafpan. Bake at 350° for 1 hour or until a wooden pick inserted in center comes out clean. Cool in pan on a wire rack 10 minutes. Remove from pan, and let cool completely on wire rack. Yield: 1 loaf.

You'll enjoy the tropical flair macadamia nuts add to this banana bread. If you don't have macadamias, you can substitute an equal amount of any type nut.

CRANBERRY-PUMPKIN BREAD

3½ cups all-purpose flour
1 teaspoon baking powder
2 teaspoons baking soda
¾ teaspoon salt
1⅔ cups sugar
2 teaspoons pumpkin pie spice
1 (16-ounce) can whole-berry
  cranberry sauce

1 (15-ounce) can pumpkin
4 large eggs, lightly beaten
⅔ cup vegetable oil
¾ cup chopped walnuts
Orange Glaze

Combine first 6 ingredients in a large bowl; make a well in center of mixture.
   Combine cranberry sauce and next 3 ingredients; add to dry ingredients, stirring just until blended. Stir in walnuts. Pour batter into two greased 9- x 5- x 3-inch loafpans.
   Bake at 350° for 1 hour or until a wooden pick inserted in center comes out clean. Cool in pans on wire racks 10 minutes; remove from pans, and let cool completely on wire racks. Drizzle with Orange Glaze. Yield: 2 loaves.

Lightly drizzled with a sweet orange glaze, this moist loaf bread features fall's harvest of tart cranberries, pumpkin, and walnuts. You'll find it pictured on page 105.

ORANGE GLAZE

1 cup sifted powdered sugar
¼ cup frozen orange juice
  concentrate, thawed

⅛ teaspoon ground allspice

Combine all ingredients in a small bowl, and stir until smooth. Yield: ½ cup.

Strawberry Jam Coffee Cake

1 (8-ounce) package cream cheese, softened
½ cup butter, softened
¾ cup sugar
2 large eggs, lightly beaten
¼ cup milk
1 teaspoon vanilla extract
2 cups all-purpose flour

1 teaspoon baking powder
½ teaspoon baking soda
¼ teaspoon salt
1 (18-ounce) jar strawberry preserves
1 tablespoon lemon juice
½ cup chopped pecans
¼ cup firmly packed brown sugar

Beat cream cheese and butter at medium speed of an electric mixer until creamy; gradually add ¾ cup sugar, beating well. Combine eggs, milk, and vanilla; add to cream cheese mixture. Beat well.

Combine flour and next 3 ingredients; add to cream cheese mixture, mixing at low speed until blended. Spoon half of batter into a greased and floured 13- x 9- x 2-inch pan. Combine strawberry preserves and lemon juice; spread over batter in pan. Dollop remaining batter over strawberry mixture. Combine pecans and brown sugar; sprinkle over batter in pan.

Bake at 350° for 35 minutes or until a wooden pick inserted in center comes out clean. Let cool 15 minutes before serving. Cut cake into squares to serve. Yield: 15 servings.

Pumpkin Pancakes

Create a new breakfast or brunch sensation with these spiced pumpkin pancakes.

2 cups all-purpose flour
1 tablespoon plus 1 teaspoon baking powder
1 teaspoon salt
2 tablespoons sugar
1 teaspoon ground cinnamon or pumpkin pie spice

4 large eggs, separated
1½ cups milk
1 cup canned pumpkin
½ cup butter or margarine, melted

Combine first 5 ingredients in a large bowl; make a well in center of mixture.

Combine egg yolks, milk, pumpkin, and butter; add to flour mixture, stirring just until dry ingredients are moistened.

Beat egg whites at high speed of an electric mixer until stiff peaks form. Gently fold beaten egg white into pumpkin mixture.

Pour about ¼ cup batter for each pancake onto a hot, lightly greased griddle. Cook pancakes until tops are covered with bubbles and edges look cooked; turn and cook other side. Yield: 24 (4-inch) pancakes.

OUT-OF-THIS-WORLD PECAN WAFFLES

2½ cups all-purpose flour
1 tablespoon plus 1 teaspoon baking powder
¾ teaspoon salt
1½ tablespoons sugar
2 large eggs, beaten

2¼ cups milk
¾ cup vegetable oil
½ cup very finely chopped pecans
¼ cup coarsely chopped pecans
Maple syrup (optional)
Whipped cream (optional)

Combine first 4 ingredients in a large bowl. Combine eggs, milk, and oil; add to flour mixture, stirring just until moistened. Stir in finely chopped pecans.

Bake in a preheated, oiled waffle iron until golden. Serve with coarsely chopped pecans; if desired, top with syrup and whipped cream. Yield: 22 (4-inch) waffles.

EASY BUTTERY CRESCENT ROLLS

You can chill this dough up to three days, and cut and shape as much as you need when you need it. The rolls bake up extra light and buttery. This convenient do-ahead bread is pictured on page 8.

1 package active dry yeast
1 cup warm water (105° to 115°), divided
1 teaspoon sugar
1 cup butter or margarine, softened

½ cup sugar
½ teaspoon salt
2 large eggs
4 to 4½ cups all-purpose flour

Combine yeast, ¼ cup water, and 1 teaspoon sugar in a 1-cup liquid measuring cup; let stand 5 minutes.

Combine yeast mixture, remaining ¾ cup warm water, butter, and next 3 ingredients in a large mixing bowl; beat at medium speed of an electric mixer until well blended. Gradually stir in enough flour to make a soft dough. Place dough in a well-greased bowl, turning to grease top. Cover and chill at least 3 hours or up to 3 days.

Turn dough out onto a heavily floured surface, and knead lightly 4 or 5 times. Divide dough into fourths; shape each portion into a ball. Roll each ball into an 11-inch circle on a lightly floured surface. Cut each circle into 8 wedges; roll up each wedge, beginning at the wide end. Place on ungreased baking sheets, point side down. Cover and let rise in a warm place (85°), free from drafts, 30 minutes or until doubled in bulk. Bake at 375° for 14 to 16 minutes or until golden. Yield: 32 rolls.

BASIL BATTER ROLLS

These pesto-flavored batter rolls couldn't be easier—no kneading!

2 packages active dry yeast
1½ cups warm water (105° to 115°)
⅓ cup shortening
4 cups unbleached flour
¼ cup sugar

1½ teaspoons salt
1 large egg
2 tablespoons pesto
2 cloves garlic, minced
Melted butter or margarine (optional)

Combine yeast and warm water in a 2-cup liquid measuring cup; let stand 5 minutes.

Combine yeast mixture, shortening, 2 cups flour, and next 3 ingredients in a large mixing bowl; beat at medium speed of an electric mixer until well blended. Stir in pesto and garlic. Gradually stir in enough remaining flour to make a soft dough. (Dough will be sticky.)

Cover and let rise in a warm place (85°), free from drafts, 50 minutes or until doubled in bulk.

Stir dough; spoon into greased muffin pans, filling half full. Cover and let rise in a warm place, free from drafts, 45 minutes.

Bake at 400° for 15 to 16 minutes or until golden. Brush with melted butter, if desired. Yield: 2 dozen.

ORANGE COFFEE ROLLS

1 package active dry yeast
¼ cup warm water (105° to 115°)
1 cup sugar, divided
2 large eggs
½ cup sour cream
¼ cup plus 2 tablespoons butter or
 margarine, melted
1 teaspoon salt

2¾ to 3 cups all-purpose flour
2 tablespoons butter or margarine,
 melted and divided
1 cup flaked coconut, toasted and
 divided
2 tablespoons grated orange rind
Glaze

Combine yeast and warm water in a large mixing bowl; let stand 5 minutes. Add ¼ cup sugar, eggs, and next 3 ingredients; beat at medium speed of an electric mixer until blended. Gradually stir in enough flour to make a soft dough.

Turn dough out onto a well-floured surface, and knead until smooth and elastic (about 5 minutes). Place in a well-greased bowl, turning to grease top. Cover and let rise in a warm place (85°), free from drafts, 1½ hours or until doubled in bulk.

Punch dough down, and divide in half. Roll 1 portion of dough into a 12-inch circle; brush with 1 tablespoon melted butter. Combine remaining ¾ cup sugar, ¾ cup coconut, and orange rind; sprinkle half of coconut mixture over dough. Cut into 12 wedges; roll up each wedge, beginning at wide end. Place in a greased 13- x 9- x 2-inch pan, point side down. Repeat with remaining dough, butter, and coconut mixture.

Cover and let rise in a warm place, free from drafts, 45 minutes or until doubled in bulk. Bake at 350° for 25 to 30 minutes or until golden. (Cover with aluminum foil after 15 minutes to prevent excessive browning, if necessary.) Spoon warm Glaze over warm rolls; sprinkle with remaining ¼ cup coconut. Yield: 2 dozen.

GLAZE

¾ cup sugar
½ cup sour cream

¼ cup butter or margarine
2 teaspoons orange juice

Combine all ingredients in a small saucepan; bring to a boil. Boil 3 minutes, stirring occasionally. Let cool slightly. Yield: about 1⅓ cups.

SOUR CREAM CINNAMON BUNS

Our Test Kitchens staff gave these yummy buns its highest rating. See them on page 104.

1 (8-ounce) carton sour cream
2 tablespoons butter or margarine
3 tablespoons sugar
½ teaspoon salt
⅛ teaspoon baking soda
1 large egg, lightly beaten
1 package active dry yeast

3 cups all-purpose flour, divided
2 tablespoons butter or margarine, softened
½ cup firmly packed brown sugar
2 teaspoons ground cinnamon
1½ cups sifted powdered sugar
2 tablespoons milk

Heat sour cream in a small saucepan over medium-low heat to 105° to 115°.

Combine warm sour cream, 2 tablespoons butter, and next 3 ingredients in a large mixing bowl. Add egg and yeast; blend well. Add 1½ cups flour; beat at medium speed of an electric mixer until well blended. Gradually stir in enough remaining 1½ cups flour to make a soft dough.

Turn dough out onto a lightly floured surface, and knead lightly 4 or 5 times. Cover and let rest 5 minutes.

Roll dough into an 18- x 6-inch rectangle; spread 2 tablespoons softened butter over dough. Sprinkle brown sugar and cinnamon over dough. Roll up dough, starting at long side, pressing firmly to eliminate air pockets; pinch seam to seal.

Slice roll into 12 (1½-inch) slices. Place slices, cut side down, in greased muffin pans. Cover and let rise in a warm place (85°), free from drafts, 30 minutes or until doubled in bulk. Bake at 375° for 12 to 15 minutes or until lightly golden. Remove buns from pan immediately; let cool on a wire rack. Combine powdered sugar and milk; drizzle over buns. Yield: 1 dozen.

HONEY-CINNAMON-CURRANT BREAD

2 packages active dry yeast
2¼ cups warm water (105° to 115°)
2 cups whole wheat flour
4 cups unbleached flour, divided
½ cup instant nonfat dry milk powder

2 tablespoons brown sugar
1 tablespoon salt
1 tablespoon ground cinnamon
⅓ cup vegetable oil
¼ cup honey
¾ cup currants

Combine yeast and warm water in a large mixing bowl; let stand 5 minutes. Add whole wheat flour, 2 cups unbleached flour, dry milk powder, and next 5 ingredients to yeast mixture; beat at medium speed of an electric mixer until well blended. Gradually stir in enough remaining unbleached flour to make a soft dough. Stir in currants.

Cover dough, and let rise in a warm place (85°), free from drafts, 15 minutes.

Punch dough down; turn out onto a lightly floured surface, and knead lightly 4 or 5 times. Divide dough in half. Roll 1 portion of dough into a 14- x 7-inch rectangle. Roll up dough, starting at short side, pressing firmly to eliminate air pockets; pinch ends to seal. Place dough, seam side down, in a well-greased 9- x 5- x 3-inch loafpan. Repeat procedure with remaining portion of dough.

Cover and let rise in a warm place, free from drafts, 1 hour or until doubled in bulk. Bake at 350° for 30 minutes or until loaves sound hollow when tapped. Remove bread from pans immediately; let cool on wire racks. Yield: 2 loaves.

CHRISTMAS MORNING BREAD

2 cups milk	2 packages active dry yeast
½ cup shortening	2 large eggs
7 to 7½ cups all-purpose flour	1 tablespoon ground cinnamon
1¾ cups sugar, divided	½ cup butter or margarine, melted
2 teaspoons salt	1 cup raisins

Combine milk and shortening in a saucepan; heat until shortening melts, stirring occasionally. Cool to 120° to 130°.

Combine 2 cups flour, ½ cup sugar, salt, and yeast in a large mixing bowl. Gradually add milk mixture to flour mixture, beating at low speed of an electric mixer. Beat 2 more minutes at medium speed. Add eggs; beat well. Gradually stir in enough remaining flour to make a soft dough.

Turn dough out onto a floured surface, and knead until smooth and elastic (about 5 minutes). Place in a well-greased bowl, turning to grease top. Cover and let rise in a warm place (85°), free from drafts, 1 hour or until doubled in bulk.

Combine remaining 1¼ cups sugar and cinnamon; set aside.

Punch dough down; turn out onto a lightly floured surface, and knead lightly 4 or 5 times. Divide dough into fourths. Shape 1 portion of dough into 1½-inch balls, keeping remaining dough covered; dip balls in melted butter, and roll in sugar-cinnamon mixture. Place balls in a greased 12-cup Bundt pan or 10-inch tube pan; sprinkle with ¼ cup raisins. Repeat procedure with second portion of dough and ¼ cup raisins. Press balls lightly to level. Set pan aside.

Repeat procedure, using another greased pan, remaining dough, sugar-cinnamon mixture, and raisins. Cover pans; let dough rise in a warm place, free from drafts, 45 minutes or until doubled in bulk. Bake at 350° for 30 to 35 minutes or until golden. Invert immediately onto serving plates; serve warm. Yield: 2 loaves.

Plump raisins freckle this cinnamon- and sugar-glazed loaf, also called monkey bread. You can make it ahead, wrap in foil, and freeze it up to a month. Thaw in foil; reheat, wrapped, at 350° for 20 minutes.

Cranberry-Apple-Filled Walnut
Cake Roll (page 122)

Heavenly Delights

Chocolate-Macadamia Pie (page 125)

BOURBON-LACED FRUIT AND NUT CAKE

Yes, this cake calls for a dozen eggs, but every rich bite is worth it!

1 cup butter or margarine, softened
2 cups sugar
3½ cups sifted cake flour
3½ teaspoons baking powder
¾ teaspoon salt
1 cup milk
1 teaspoon vanilla extract
8 egg whites
Fruit Filling
Frosting

Grease four 9-inch round cakepans; line with wax paper. Grease wax paper, and set aside.

Beat butter at medium speed of an electric mixer until creamy; gradually add sugar, beating well.

Combine flour, baking powder, and salt; add to butter mixture alternately with milk, beginning and ending with flour mixture. Mix at low speed after each addition until blended. Stir in vanilla.

Beat egg whites at high speed until stiff peaks form. Gently fold into flour mixture. Pour batter into prepared pans.

Bake at 375° for 20 minutes or until a wooden pick inserted in center comes out clean. Cool in pans on wire racks 10 minutes; remove from pans, and let cool completely on wire racks.

Spread Fruit Filling between layers and on top of cake. Spread Frosting on sides of cake. Yield: one 4-layer cake.

FRUIT FILLING

1½ cups raisins
1½ cups red candied cherries, quartered
1½ cups pecans, coarsely chopped
1½ cups flaked coconut
12 egg yolks, lightly beaten
1¾ cups sugar
¾ cup butter
½ teaspoon salt
½ cup bourbon

Place raisins in a small saucepan, and cover with water. Bring to a boil; cover, remove from heat, and let stand 5 minutes. Drain and pat dry. Combine raisins, cherries, chopped pecans, and coconut in a large bowl; set aside.

Combine egg yolks, sugar, butter, and salt in top of a double boiler; bring water to a boil. Reduce heat to medium; cook, stirring constantly, 20 minutes or until mixture is very thick. Add bourbon; stir well. Pour over fruit mixture, stirring well; let cool completely. Yield: enough for one 4-layer cake.

FROSTING

1½ cups sugar
½ teaspoon cream of tartar
½ cup water
4 egg whites
½ teaspoon vanilla extract

Combine first 3 ingredients in a heavy saucepan. Cook over medium heat, stirring constantly, until mixture is clear. Cook, without stirring, until mixture reaches soft ball stage or until candy thermometer registers 240°. While syrup cooks, beat egg whites until soft peaks form; continue to beat, adding syrup in a heavy stream. Add vanilla; continue beating just until stiff peaks form and frosting is thick enough to spread. Immediately spread frosting on cake. Yield: 7 cups.

TRIPLE CHOCOLATE ECSTASY

4 (1-ounce) squares semisweet
  chocolate
½ cup butter or margarine
1 cup finely chopped pecans
2 large eggs, lightly beaten
2 cups sugar
1½ cups all-purpose flour

1 teaspoon baking powder
½ teaspoon salt
1½ cups milk
1 teaspoon vanilla extract
Chocolate Filling
Chocolate Frosting

Grease two 9-inch round cakepans; line with wax paper. Grease wax paper, and set aside.

Combine chocolate and butter in a heavy saucepan. Cook over low heat, stirring often, until chocolate melts. Add pecans; stir well. Remove from heat.

Combine eggs and sugar. Stir in chocolate mixture. Combine flour, baking powder, and salt; add to chocolate mixture alternately with milk, beginning and ending with flour mixture. Stir in vanilla. Pour batter into prepared pans.

Bake at 350° for 45 to 48 minutes or until a wooden pick inserted in center comes out clean. Cool in pans on wire racks 5 minutes; remove from pans, and let cool completely on wire racks.

Spread Chocolate Filling between layers of cake. Spread Chocolate Frosting on top and sides of cake. Yield: one 2-layer cake.

CHOCOLATE FILLING

4 (1-ounce) squares semisweet
  chocolate
¼ cup butter or margarine

½ cup sifted powdered sugar
⅓ cup milk

Combine chocolate and butter in a heavy saucepan. Cook over low heat, stirring often, until chocolate melts. Gradually add powdered sugar alternately with milk, beginning and ending with powdered sugar; stir until smooth. Cover and chill 30 minutes or until spreading consistency. Yield: 1 cup.

CHOCOLATE FROSTING

2 cups whipping cream
1 cup sifted powdered sugar

⅔ cup sifted cocoa
1 teaspoon vanilla extract

Combine all ingredients in a bowl; beat at high speed of an electric mixer until stiff peaks form. Yield: 4 cups.

WHITE CHOCOLATE POINSETTIA CAKE

You'll wow guests when you present this cake (pictured on cover) at your holiday gathering. White chocolate flavors and garnishes the cake beautifully. Regular white chocolate baking bars (we tested with Baker's) work best in the layers and frosting, while block white chocolate from a candy counter produces the smoothest, prettiest leaves.

2 ounces premium white chocolate baking bar, chopped (we tested with Baker's)

¼ cup plus 1 tablespoon white crème de cacao

½ cup butter, softened

2 tablespoons shortening

1¼ cups sugar

3 large eggs

1¾ cups all-purpose flour

¾ teaspoon baking soda

½ teaspoon baking powder

¾ cup buttermilk

White Chocolate Buttercream Frosting

1 (9-ounce) jar low-calorie cranberry-raspberry preserves, divided (we tested with Knotts Light Preserves)

White Chocolate Poinsettia Leaves

Fresh cranberries

Place white chocolate in a 1-cup liquid measuring cup; microwave at HIGH 2 minutes or until chocolate melts, stirring once. Add crème de cacao, mixing well; cool.

Beat butter and shortening at medium speed of an electric mixer until creamy; gradually add sugar, beating well. Add eggs, one at a time, beating after each addition.

Combine flour, baking soda, and baking powder; add to butter mixture alternately with buttermilk, beginning and ending with flour mixture. Mix at low speed after each addition until blended. Stir in white chocolate mixture. Pour batter into three greased and floured 8-inch round cakepans.

Bake at 350° for 16 to 18 minutes or until a wooden pick inserted in center comes out clean. Cool in pans on wire racks 10 minutes; remove from pans, and let cool completely on wire racks.

Place 1 cake layer on a pedestal cake stand; spread 1 cup frosting and then half of preserves on first cake layer; top with a second cake layer. Spread 1 cup frosting and then remaining preserves on second cake layer; top with remaining cake layer. Spread remaining frosting on top and sides of cake. Arrange White Chocolate Poinsettia Leaves on top of cake, forming 1 large flower; arrange any remaining leaves around cake stand. Garnish with fresh cranberries. Yield: 1 (3-layer cake).

WHITE CHOCOLATE BUTTERCREAM FROSTING

½ cup plus 1 tablespoon whipping cream

1 (6-ounce) premium white chocolate baking bar, finely chopped (we tested with Baker's)

¼ cup plus 2 tablespoons white crème de cacao

1½ cups unsalted butter, softened

6½ cups sifted powdered sugar

Bring whipping cream to a boil in a small heavy saucepan over medium-high heat; remove from heat, and add white chocolate, stirring until chocolate is melted and smooth. Add crème de cacao, stirring until blended. Cool completely, stirring occasionally. Beat butter at medium speed of an electric mixer until creamy. Gradually add sugar; beat until blended. Gradually add cooled chocolate mixture, beating until spreading consistency. Yield: 5¼ cups.

WHITE CHOCOLATE POINSETTIA LEAVES

8 ounces high-quality block white chocolate, finely chopped (we tested with white chocolate from a candy store)

Red decorating gel (we tested with Betty Crocker)
20 lemon or camellia leaves, washed and dried

Line two baking sheets with wax paper; set aside. Place chocolate in top of a double boiler; place over hot water, stirring just until melted and smooth. Place 1 tablespoon melted chocolate in a small bowl; add a tiny amount of food coloring, stirring until tinted pale pink. Add additional white chocolate if pink is too dark.

Using a small brush, paint delicate strokes of pink chocolate down center of back of 1 leaf, feathering outward and following veins of leaf (photo 1). Immediately spread a ⅛-inch layer of white chocolate over entire back of leaf, gently spreading outward from center to marbleize color (photo 2). Place leaf on prepared baking sheet, chocolate side up; repeat with remaining leaves. Freeze leaves 20 minutes or until chocolate is firm. Remove from freezer. Grasp each leaf at stem end, and gently peel leaf from chocolate (photo 3). Store chocolate leaves in freezer while assembling cake. Leaves can be made several days ahead. Handle carefully because chocolate leaves are thin and will melt quickly from the heat of your hand (photo 4).

Don't let chocolate-covered poinsettia leaves intimidate you—they're quite easy. Just follow our techniques below. Lemon and camellia leaves are nontoxic and edible, which make them ideal for painting with chocolate. Be sure not to use leaves that have been sprayed with pesticide. Your best bet if you don't have any of these leaves is to get them from a neighbor (who you know hasn't sprayed them with pesticide) rather than a florist.

1. Paint delicate strokes of pink chocolate down center of back of leaf, feathering outward and following veins of leaf.

2. Immediately spread a layer of white chocolate over entire back of leaf, gently spreading outward from center to marbleize color.

3. Grasp frozen leaf at stem end, and gently peel leaf from chocolate.

4. Handle leaves carefully because they are thin and melt quickly from the heat of your hand. Store leaves in freezer while assembling cake.

ORANGE-RUM CAKE

This cake's even better the second day. Let the cake soak up the rum syrup overnight for a spirited delight.

½ cup fresh orange juice
½ cup light rum
⅔ cup butter or margarine, softened
1½ cups sugar
4 large eggs
2½ cups all-purpose flour

2 teaspoons baking powder
½ teaspoon baking soda
2 tablespoons grated orange rind
1 cup chopped pecans
Orange-Rum Syrup

Combine orange juice and rum; set aside.

Beat butter at medium speed of an electric mixer 2 minutes or until creamy. Gradually add sugar, beating at medium speed 5 to 7 minutes. Add eggs, one at a time, beating just until yellow disappears.

Combine flour, baking powder, and soda; add to butter mixture alternately with orange juice mixture. Mix at low speed just until blended after each addition. Stir in orange rind. Sprinkle pecans in bottom of a heavily buttered and floured 12-cup Bundt pan. Pour batter evenly over pecans.

Bake at 325° for 1 hour or until a wooden pick inserted in center comes out clean. Cool in pan on a wire rack 10 to 15 minutes; invert pan onto wire rack to loosen cake from pan. Immediately return cake to pan.

Prick cake to bottom of pan at 1-inch intervals with a long wooden skewer or cake tester. Spoon Orange-Rum Syrup over warm cake. Cool at least 3 hours in pan. Remove cake from pan to serve. Yield: one 10-inch cake.

ORANGE-RUM SYRUP

½ cup sugar
2 tablespoons butter or margarine, melted

1 tablespoon grated orange rind
2 tablespoons fresh orange juice
2 tablespoons light rum

Combine all ingredients; stir until sugar dissolves. Yield: about ⅔ cup.

COCONUT-CREAM CHEESE POUND CAKE

Fans of macaroons will enjoy the rich coconut flavor of this pound cake.

½ cup butter or margarine, softened
½ cup shortening
1 (8-ounce) package cream cheese, softened
3 cups sugar
6 large eggs
3 cups all-purpose flour

¼ teaspoon baking soda
¼ teaspoon salt
1 (6-ounce) package frozen grated fresh coconut, thawed
1 teaspoon vanilla extract
1 teaspoon coconut extract

Beat first 3 ingredients at medium speed of an electric mixer 2 minutes or until soft and creamy; gradually add sugar, beating at medium speed 5 to 7 minutes. Add eggs, one at a time, beating just until yellow disappears.

Combine flour, soda, and salt; add to butter mixture. Mix at low speed just until blended. Stir in coconut and flavorings. Pour batter into a greased and floured 10-inch tube pan.

Bake at 350° for 1 hour and 30 minutes or until a wooden pick inserted in center comes out clean. Cool in pan on a wire rack 15 minutes; remove from pan, and cool completely on wire rack. Yield: one 10-inch cake.

GINGERBREAD

½ cup shortening
½ cup sugar
2 large eggs
½ cup molasses
1½ cups all-purpose flour
1 teaspoon baking soda

1 teaspoon ground cinnamon
1 teaspoon ground allspice
1 teaspoon ground ginger
1 cup hot water
Whipped cream
Ground cinnamon (optional)

Hot from the oven, this moist cake demands a dollop of whipped cream and a fork. And if there's any left over, enjoy a glass of milk with this spiced snack cake.

Beat shortening at medium speed of an electric mixer until light and fluffy; gradually add sugar, beating well. Add eggs and molasses, mixing well.

Combine flour and next 4 ingredients; add to shortening mixture alternately with water, beginning and ending with flour mixture. Mix after each addition. Pour batter into a greased and floured 8-inch square pan.

Bake at 350° for 30 minutes or until a wooden pick inserted in center of cake comes out clean. Serve cake dolloped with whipped cream, and sprinkle with ground cinnamon, if desired. Yield: 9 servings.

CRANBERRY-APPLE-FILLED WALNUT CAKE ROLL

This cake roll is filled with the ingredients of the season—apples, cranberries, and walnuts—with sprinklings of cinnamon and nutmeg. Find it pictured on page 114.

2 large cooking apples, peeled, cored, and chopped
1 cup fresh cranberries
¼ cup sugar
¼ cup water
2 tablespoons brandy
1 teaspoon lemon juice
½ teaspoon ground cinnamon
¼ teaspoon ground nutmeg
⅔ cup all-purpose flour
1 teaspoon baking powder

¼ teaspoon salt
3 large eggs
¾ cup sugar
⅓ cup water
1 teaspoon vanilla extract
⅓ cup ground walnuts
2 to 3 tablespoons powdered sugar
1½ cups whipping cream
½ teaspoon ground cinnamon
1 teaspoon vanilla extract
Garnish: coarsely chopped walnuts

Coat a 15- x 10- x 1-inch jellyroll pan with cooking spray. Line bottom of pan with wax paper; coat wax paper with cooking spray. Set aside.

Combine first 8 ingredients in a medium saucepan. Cook over medium heat about 10 minutes or until cranberry skins pop and liquid is absorbed, stirring occasionally. Let cool completely.

Combine flour, baking powder, and salt; set aside. Beat eggs in a large mixing bowl at high speed of an electric mixer 2 minutes. Gradually add ¾ cup sugar, beating 5 minutes or until thick and pale. Stir in ⅓ cup water and 1 teaspoon vanilla. Gradually fold flour mixture and ground walnuts into egg mixture with a wire whisk. Spread batter evenly in prepared pan. Bake at 375° for 12 minutes or until cake springs back when lightly touched in the center.

Sift powdered sugar in a 15- x 10-inch rectangle on a cloth towel. When cake is done, immediately loosen from sides of pan, and turn out onto towel. Peel off wax paper. Starting at narrow end, roll up cake and towel together; place, seam side down, on a wire rack to cool.

Unroll cake; spread with cranberry mixture. Reroll cake without towel; place, seam side down, on a serving plate.

Beat whipping cream, ½ teaspoon ground cinnamon, and 1 teaspoon vanilla at high speed until stiff peaks form. Spread mixture over cake, or, if desired, pipe it over cake. To pipe it, spoon mixture into a decorating bag fitted with a large flower tip (we used Wilton No. 1E), and pipe icing in strips to cover cake. Garnish, if desired. Yield: 1 cake roll (6 servings).

CRANBERRY-APPLE-CHEESE PIE

1 unbaked 9-inch pastry shell
1 (8-ounce) package cream cheese, softened
⅓ cup firmly packed brown sugar
2½ tablespoons cornstarch
⅛ teaspoon salt
1 (16-ounce) can whole-berry cranberry sauce
2 cups peeled and thinly sliced Rome Beauty or other tart cooking apple
Walnut Streusel Topping

Line pastry shell with aluminum foil or wax paper, and fill with pie weights or dried beans.

Bake at 425° for 15 minutes. Remove foil, and bake 5 more minutes. Cool completely on a wire rack.

Beat cream cheese in a small mixing bowl at medium speed of an electric mixer until creamy. Spread evenly on bottom of pastry shell.

Combine brown sugar, cornstarch, and salt; add cranberry sauce and apple, stirring gently. Spoon evenly over cream cheese; sprinkle with Walnut Streusel Topping. Bake at 375° for 45 minutes. (Cover edges of pastry with strips of aluminum foil to prevent excessive browning after 15 minutes.) Cool on wire rack. Yield: one 9-inch pie.

WALNUT STREUSEL TOPPING

½ cup chopped walnuts
⅓ cup all-purpose flour
3 tablespoons firmly packed brown sugar
¼ teaspoon ground cinnamon
¼ cup butter or margarine

Combine first 4 ingredients in a bowl. Cut in butter with pastry blender until mixture is crumbly. Yield: 1½ cups.

PEPPERMINT PIE

If you can't find peppermint ice cream, substitute mint chocolate chip ice cream. If your grocery store doesn't carry either flavor, it's worth a trip to your favorite ice cream parlor.

2 cups (12 ounces) semisweet
  chocolate morsels, divided
¼ cup plus 2 tablespoons butter or
  margarine, divided
2 cups crisp rice cereal

½ cup chopped walnuts, toasted
1 quart peppermint ice cream,
  softened
½ cup milk
Crushed hard peppermint candy

Cook 1 cup chocolate morsels and 2 tablespoons butter in a large heavy saucepan over low heat until chocolate and butter melt, stirring occasionally. Remove from heat. Stir in cereal and walnuts. Firmly press cereal mixture in bottom and up sides of a greased 9-inch pieplate. Chill until firm.

Spoon softened ice cream into prepared crust. Cover and freeze until firm.

Combine remaining 1 cup chocolate morsels, remaining ¼ cup butter, and milk in a small heavy saucepan. Cook over low heat, stirring constantly, until chocolate and butter melt. Set aside, and let cool.

Let pie stand at room temperature 5 minutes before serving. To serve, spoon chocolate mixture evenly over pie slices, and sprinkle with crushed candy. Yield: one 9-inch pie.

CHOCOLATE-MACADAMIA PIE

4 large eggs, lightly beaten
¾ cup light corn syrup
½ cup firmly packed brown sugar
¼ cup butter or margarine, melted
2 teaspoons Kahlúa or other coffee-
   flavored liqueur

2 teaspoons vanilla extract
1 cup (6 ounces) semisweet chocolate
   morsels
1 (7-ounce) jar macadamia nuts
1 unbaked 9-inch pastry shell
Coffee Cream (optional)

If you aren't a macadamia nut fan, try substituting pecans in this luscious mocha-flavored pie. See it on page 115.

Combine first 6 ingredients in a medium bowl; stir well. Stir in chocolate morsels and nuts.

Pour into pastry shell; bake at 425° for 10 minutes. Reduce oven temperature to 350°, and bake 30 more minutes or until set. (Cover edges of pastry with strips of aluminum foil to prevent excessive browning, if necessary.) Cool completely on a wire rack; cover and chill thoroughly. Dollop Coffee Cream on top of pie, if desired. Chill 30 minutes. Yield: one 9-inch pie.

COFFEE CREAM

1 cup whipping cream
2 tablespoons powdered sugar

2 tablespoons Kahlúa or other coffee
   flavored liqueur

Combine all ingredients in a small mixing bowl; beat at high speed of an electric mixer until stiff peaks form. Yield: 2 cups.

COOL WHITE CHOCOLATE-PECAN PIE

2 tablespoons butter or margarine
2 cups chopped pecans
8 ounces white chocolate, broken
   into pieces
¼ cup milk

2 cups whipping cream
½ cup sugar
1 tablespoon vanilla extract
1 baked 9-inch pastry shell

Chunky pecans wade in a velvety sea of white chocolate whipped cream.

Melt butter in a large skillet over medium-high heat. Add pecans, and cook until toasted, stirring often. Let cool completely on paper towels.

Position knife blade in food processor bowl; add chocolate pieces. Process until finely chopped. Combine chocolate and milk in a heavy saucepan; cook over low heat, stirring constantly, until chocolate melts. Let cool.

Beat whipping cream until foamy; gradually add sugar and vanilla, beating until soft peaks form. Fold in chocolate mixture and pecans.

Spoon filling into pastry shell. Cover and chill at least 3 hours. Yield: one 9-inch pie.

Cinnamon Custard Pie

Small- or large-curd cottage cheese will work equally well in this old-fashioned pie.

2 cups cottage cheese
¼ cup milk
1 cup sugar
3 large eggs, lightly beaten
1 tablespoon all-purpose flour

1 teaspoon vanilla extract
⅛ teaspoon salt
1 unbaked 9-inch pastry shell
1 teaspoon sugar
½ teaspoon ground cinnamon

Combine cottage cheese and milk in container of an electric blender; process until smooth, stopping once to scrape down sides.

Combine cottage cheese mixture, 1 cup sugar, and next 4 ingredients in a medium bowl; stir well. Pour into pastry shell.

Combine 1 teaspoon sugar and cinnamon; stir well. Sprinkle over cottage cheese mixture. Bake at 450° for 5 minutes. Reduce oven temperature to 350°, and bake 25 more minutes or until a knife inserted in center comes out clean. Serve warm or at room temperature. Yield: one 9-inch pie.

Sweet Potato Pie with Praline Crust

A buttery praline layer baked in the crust elevates this classic sweet potato pie to a new level.

1⅓ cups all-purpose flour
½ teaspoon salt
½ cup shortening
3 to 4 tablespoons cold water
3 tablespoons butter or margarine, softened
⅓ cup firmly packed dark brown sugar
⅓ cup chopped pecans
3 large eggs, lightly beaten
1 cup evaporated milk

1½ cups cooked, mashed sweet potato
½ cup sugar
½ cup firmly packed dark brown sugar
1 teaspoon salt
1 teaspoon ground cinnamon
¼ teaspoon ground cloves
¼ teaspoon ground nutmeg
Whipped cream (optional)

Combine flour and ½ teaspoon salt; cut in shortening with a pastry blender until mixture is crumbly. Sprinkle cold water (1 tablespoon at a time) evenly over surface; stir with a fork until dry ingredients are moistened. Shape into a ball; cover and chill.

Roll dough into a 12-inch circle on a lightly floured surface. Place in a 10-inch pieplate; trim off excess pastry along edges. Fold edges under, and flute.

Combine butter and ⅓ cup brown sugar; stir in pecans. Press mixture over pastry shell. Bake at 425° for 5 minutes. Let cool on a wire rack. Reduce oven temperature to 350°.

Combine eggs and next 8 ingredients in a large mixing bowl; beat at medium speed of an electric mixer until blended. Pour mixture over praline layer in pastry shell. Bake at 350° for 50 minutes or until pie is set. Let cool on wire rack. Top with whipped cream, if desired. Yield: one 10-inch pie.

Walnut Tart

⅓ cup butter or margarine, softened
¼ cup sugar
1 egg yolk
1 cup all-purpose flour
2 cups coarsely chopped walnuts, toasted

⅔ cup firmly packed brown sugar
¼ cup butter or margarine
¼ cup dark corn syrup
1 cup whipping cream, divided

Beat ⅓ cup butter and ¼ cup sugar at medium speed of an electric mixer until light and fluffy. Add egg yolk; beat well. Gradually add flour, mixing at low speed until blended. (Mixture will be crumbly.) Shape into a ball. Press pastry in bottom and up sides of a 9-inch tart pan with removable bottom. Bake at 375° for 12 minutes or until lightly browned. Cool on a wire rack.

Sprinkle walnuts evenly in bottom of tart shell. Combine brown sugar, ¼ cup butter, corn syrup, and 2 tablespoons whipping cream in a saucepan; bring to a boil over medium heat, stirring constantly. Boil 1 minute, stirring constantly. Pour over walnuts. Bake at 375° for 13 minutes or until bubbly. Cool completely in pan on wire rack.

To serve, carefully remove sides of pan. Beat remaining whipping cream until stiff peaks form. Serve tart with whipped cream. Yield: one 9-inch tart.

Pear-Cranberry Crisp

8 firm ripe pears, peeled, cored, and sliced (about 3 pounds)
2 (12-ounce) packages fresh or frozen cranberries, thawed
⅔ cup sugar
1 teaspoon ground cinnamon, divided

1½ cups regular oats, uncooked
1⅓ cups firmly packed brown sugar
1 cup all-purpose flour
Pinch of salt
1 cup butter or margarine, cut into ½-inch pieces

Combine pear slices, cranberries, ⅔ cup sugar, and ½ teaspoon cinnamon in a large bowl; toss gently. Spoon mixture into a lightly greased 13- x 9- x 2-inch baking dish.

Combine oats, brown sugar, flour, salt, and remaining ½ teaspoon cinnamon; cut in butter with a pastry blender until mixture is crumbly. Sprinkle over fruit mixture. Bake at 375° for 40 to 45 minutes or until topping is golden. Let stand 10 minutes. Yield: 10 servings.

Macadamia Nut Brittle
(page 137)

Eggnog Cookies
(page 132)

Goodies for Santa

Sinful Chocolate Balls
(page 136)

CHOCOLATE-HAZELNUT CLUSTERS

½ cup butter or margarine, softened
½ cup firmly packed dark brown
   sugar
½ cup sugar
1 large egg
1 teaspoon vanilla extract
1 teaspoon water

1½ cups regular oats, uncooked
¾ cup all-purpose flour
½ teaspoon baking powder
12 (1-ounce) squares bittersweet
   chocolate, coarsely chopped
½ cup hazelnuts, coarsely chopped

Beat butter at medium speed of an electric mixer until creamy; gradually add sugars, beating well. Add egg, vanilla, and water; beat well.

Combine oats, flour, and baking powder; add to butter mixture, beating well (dough will be crumbly). Stir in chocolate and hazelnuts. Cover and chill 1 hour.

Drop dough by heaping tablespoonfuls onto greased cookie sheets. Bake at 350° for 8 to 10 minutes. Cool 2 minutes on cookie sheets; remove to wire racks, and let cool completely. Yield: 2½ dozen.

OLD-TIME CINNAMON JUMBLES

Bring back fond memories of sneaking a treat from Grandma's cookie jar with these old-fashioned cookies. They have just the right hint of cinnamon and nutmeg.

¼ cup shortening
¼ cup butter or margarine,
   softened
1 cup sugar
1 large egg
¾ cup buttermilk
1 teaspoon vanilla extract

¼ teaspoon ground nutmeg
2 cups all-purpose flour
½ teaspoon baking soda
½ teaspoon salt
¼ cup sugar
½ teaspoon ground cinnamon

Beat shortening and butter at medium speed of an electric mixer until creamy; gradually add 1 cup sugar, beating well. Add egg, beating well. Add buttermilk, vanilla, and nutmeg; mix until blended.

Combine flour, soda, and salt; add to shortening mixture, beating well. Cover and chill at least 2 hours.

Drop dough by heaping teaspoonfuls onto lightly greased cookie sheets. Combine ¼ cup sugar and cinnamon; sprinkle evenly over cookies. Bake at 375° for 8 to 10 minutes. Remove to wire racks, and let cool completely. Yield: 4½ dozen.

EASY GINGER COOKIES

1 (14-ounce) package gingerbread
   mix
⅔ cup water

½ cup chunky peanut butter
½ cup raisins

Combine gingerbread mix, water, and peanut butter in a large bowl, stirring until smooth. Add raisins; stir well.

Drop dough by rounded teaspoonfuls onto greased cookie sheets. Bake at 350° for 10 to 12 minutes or until lightly browned. Cool 5 minutes on cookie sheets; remove to wire racks, and let cool completely. Yield: 3 dozen.

BEST-EVER OATMEAL COOKIES

1 cup shortening
1 cup sugar
1 cup firmly packed brown sugar
1 teaspoon almond extract
1 teaspoon vanilla extract
2 large eggs
2 cups all-purpose flour

1 teaspoon baking powder
1 teaspoon baking soda
1 teaspoon salt
2 cups regular oats, uncooked
1 cup chopped pecans
1 cup (6 ounces) semisweet chocolate morsels

Beat shortening at medium speed of an electric mixer until fluffy; gradually add sugars, beating well. Add flavorings and eggs; beat well.

Combine flour and next 4 ingredients; gradually add to shortening mixture, beating well. Stir in pecans and chocolate morsels.

Drop dough by heaping tablespoonfuls onto lightly greased cookie sheets. Bake at 350° for 10 minutes or until lightly browned. Cool slightly on cookie sheets; remove to wire racks, and cool completely. Yield: 3 dozen.

PUMPKIN CHIPPERS

2 cups all-purpose flour
1 cup (6 ounces) butterscotch morsels
1 teaspoon baking soda
¾ cup butter or margarine, softened
⅔ cup sugar
⅔ cup firmly packed brown sugar

1 large egg
½ cup canned pumpkin
1 cup quick-cooking oats, uncooked
1 (6-ounce) premium white chocolate baking bar, chopped (we tested with Baker's)
⅔ cup chopped walnuts

White chocolate chunks, butterscotch chips, and chopped walnuts make these pumpkin cookies something to write home about.

Position knife blade in food processor bowl; add flour and butterscotch morsels. Process 30 seconds or until morsels are finely ground.

Combine flour mixture and soda; stir well, and set aside.

Beat butter at medium speed of an electric mixer until creamy. Gradually add sugars, beating well. Add egg and pumpkin; beat well. Add flour mixture; beat well. Stir in oats, white chocolate, and walnuts.

Drop dough by heaping teaspoonfuls onto lightly greased cookie sheets. Bake at 350° for 12 minutes or until golden. Remove to wire racks immediately, and let cool completely. Yield: 6 dozen.

EGGNOG COOKIES

Brushing the cookie dough with an egg white mixture helps to keep the sugar crystals in place. Find these colorful cookies pictured on page 128.

1 cup butter, softened
2 cups sugar
5½ cups all-purpose flour
1 teaspoon baking soda
½ teaspoon ground nutmeg

1 cup eggnog
1 egg white, lightly beaten (optional)
1 tablespoon water (optional)
Colored sugar crystals

Beat butter at medium speed of an electric mixer until creamy; gradually add 2 cups sugar, beating well.

Combine flour, soda, and nutmeg; add to butter mixture alternately with eggnog, beginning and ending with flour mixture. Cover and chill at least 1 hour.

Divide dough in half. Work with 1 portion of dough at a time, storing remainder in refrigerator. Roll each portion of dough to ⅛-inch thickness on a lightly floured surface. Cut with a 4-inch cookie cutter; place on lightly greased cookie sheets.

Combine egg white and water in a small bowl; brush cookies with egg white mixture, if desired. Sprinkle with colored sugar. Bake at 375° for 8 to 10 minutes or until lightly browned. Cool slightly on cookie sheets; remove to wire racks, and let cool completely. Yield: 4½ dozen.

CHRISTMAS COOKIE PEPPERMINT BALLS

¾ cup butter or margarine, softened
¾ cup sugar, divided
1 egg yolk
1 teaspoon vanilla extract
2 cups sifted all-purpose flour

⅓ cup crushed hard peppermint candy
1 (8-ounce) package milk chocolate kisses

Beat butter at medium speed of an electric mixer until creamy; gradually add ¼ cup sugar, beating well. Add egg yolk and vanilla; beat well. Gradually add flour and crushed peppermint, beating well. Shape dough into 1-inch balls. Roll in remaining ½ cup sugar; place 2 inches apart on lightly greased cookie sheets. Bake at 350° for 7 minutes. Press a chocolate kiss into center of each cookie; bake 8 more minutes. Cool 1 minute on cookie sheets; remove to wire racks, and let cool completely. Yield: 3 dozen.

GERMAN VANILLA COOKIES

1 cup butter or margarine, softened
¾ cup sifted powdered sugar
1 egg yolk
1 teaspoon vanilla extract

2¼ cups all-purpose flour
Chocolate Glaze (optional)
Red currant jelly (optional)

Let the cookie dough stand 10 minutes before shaping it into balls and the dough will be less sticky and easier to handle.

Beat butter at medium speed of an electric mixer until creamy; gradually add powdered sugar, beating well. Add egg yolk and vanilla; beat well. Gradually add flour to butter mixture, beating well. Let stand 10 minutes.

Shape dough into 1-inch balls; place on ungreased cookie sheets. Press thumb into each ball of dough, leaving an indentation. Bake at 325° for 15 minutes. Remove to wire racks, and let cool completely. Spoon either Chocolate Glaze or jelly into indentation of each cookie. Yield: 4 dozen.

CHOCOLATE GLAZE

3 (1-ounce) squares semisweet
   chocolate

2 tablespoons butter or margarine
1 tablespoon light corn syrup

Combine all ingredients in a small heavy saucepan. Cook over low heat, stirring constantly, until chocolate and butter melt. Yield: ⅓ cup.

Peppercorn Cookies

You won't be able to eat just one of these seductively addictive dark shortbread cookies. Black and red pepper provide lusty spice appeal to the predominant chocolate presence.

¾ cup butter or margarine, softened
1 cup sugar
1 large egg
1½ teaspoons vanilla extract
1½ cups all-purpose flour
¾ cup cocoa

¾ teaspoon ground cinnamon
¼ teaspoon salt
⅛ teaspoon black pepper
⅛ teaspoon ground red pepper
Powdered sugar

Beat butter at medium speed of an electric mixer until creamy; gradually add 1 cup sugar, beating well. Add egg and vanilla; beat well. Combine flour and next 5 ingredients; gradually add to butter mixture, beating well.

Shape cookie dough into a 12-inch roll on a lightly floured surface. Wrap roll in wax paper, and chill at least 2 hours or until firm.

Slice dough into ¼-inch-thick slices, and place on greased cookie sheets. Bake at 375° for 8 minutes. Remove to wire racks, and let cool completely. Sift powdered sugar over tops of cookies. Yield: 4 dozen.

Slice of Spice

The logs of dough can be frozen up to 3 months. Let them thaw in the refrigerator just until they're soft enough to slice.

½ cup butter or margarine, softened
½ cup shortening
2 cups firmly packed brown sugar
2 large eggs
1 teaspoon vanilla extract
3 cups all-purpose flour
1 teaspoon baking soda

1 teaspoon cream of tartar
½ teaspoon salt
1 cup regular oats, uncooked
½ cup sugar
1 tablespoon plus 1 teaspoon ground cinnamon

Beat butter and shortening at medium speed of an electric mixer until creamy; gradually add brown sugar, beating well. Add eggs and vanilla; beat well.

Combine flour, soda, cream of tartar, and salt; add to butter mixture, beating well. Stir in oats.

Shape dough into 3 (12-inch) logs; wrap in wax paper. Freeze 1 hour.

Unwrap dough, and cut into ¼-inch slices. Combine ½ cup sugar and cinnamon. Dip each slice into sugar mixture, and place each on lightly greased cookie sheets. Bake at 350° for 9 to 11 minutes. Remove to wire racks, and let cool completely. Yield: about 7 dozen.

Chocolate-Peppermint Sticks

½ cup butter or margarine
3½ (1-ounce) squares unsweetened
   chocolate, divided
1 cup sugar
2 large eggs, lightly beaten
½ cup all-purpose flour
Dash of salt

1¾ teaspoons peppermint extract,
   divided
¼ cup butter or margarine
2 cups sifted powdered sugar
2 tablespoons whipping cream or
   half-and-half
1 tablespoon butter or margarine

For best results, chill these rich and gooey brownies before cutting them into bars.

Combine ½ cup butter and 2 squares chocolate in a large saucepan; cook over low heat until butter and chocolate melt, stirring occasionally. Gradually add 1 cup sugar and next 3 ingredients, stirring until blended. Stir in ¼ teaspoon peppermint extract.

Pour batter into a lightly greased 8-inch square pan. Bake at 350° for 24 minutes. Cool completely in pan on a wire rack.

Melt ¼ cup butter in a saucepan over low heat; stir in remaining 1½ teaspoons peppermint extract, powdered sugar, and whipping cream. Spread over brownies. Chill 15 minutes.

Combine 1 tablespoon butter and remaining 1½ squares chocolate in a small heavy saucepan; cook over low heat until butter and chocolate melt, stirring occasionally. Drizzle chocolate mixture evenly over powdered sugar mixture. Cover and chill at least 30 minutes. Cut into 2- x 1-inch bars. Yield: 32 bars.

SNOW WHITE CHOCOLATE FUDGE

2 cups sugar
¾ cup sour cream
½ cup butter or margarine
2 cups (12 ounces) vanilla-milk
   morsels

1 (7-ounce) jar marshmallow cream
1 (3.5-ounce) jar macadamia nuts,
   chopped or ¾ cup chopped walnuts

Combine first 3 ingredients in a large heavy saucepan; cook over medium heat, stirring constantly, until sugar dissolves and mixture comes to a boil. Cover and cook 2 to 3 minutes to wash down sugar crystals from sides of pan. Uncover and cook to soft ball stage (238°), without stirring.

Remove from heat; add vanilla morsels, stirring until melted. Stir in marshmallow cream and nuts. Spread mixture evenly in a buttered 8-inch square pan. Cool and cut into squares. Cover and store in refrigerator. Yield: 2¾ pounds.

FIVE-MINUTE FUDGE

Got 5 minutes to cook? You can have fudge!

1⅔ cups sugar
⅔ cup evaporated milk
½ teaspoon salt
1½ cups miniature marshmallows

1½ cups semisweet chocolate morsels
½ cup chopped pecans or walnuts
1 teaspoon vanilla extract

Combine first 3 ingredients in a large saucepan. Bring to a boil; cook 5 minutes, stirring constantly. Remove from heat; add marshmallows and remaining ingredients, stirring until marshmallows and chocolate morsels melt. Spoon mixture into a buttered 9-inch square pan, spreading evenly. Let cool completely. Cut into squares. Yield: 2 pounds.

SINFUL CHOCOLATE BALLS

Calling all chocoholics! You'll find nearly 3 pounds of your favorite vice in these devilish delights. Look for them on page 129.

1 cup plus 2 tablespoons whipping
   cream
¾ cup unsalted butter
20 (1-ounce) squares semisweet
   chocolate
¾ cup sour cream
¼ cup plus 2 tablespoons Grand
   Marnier or other orange-flavored
   liqueur

1½ tablespoons grated orange rind
½ cup sifted powdered sugar
6 (4-ounce) packages sweet baking
   chocolate

Combine whipping cream and butter in a large heavy saucepan; bring to a boil over medium heat. Remove from heat; add semisweet chocolate, stirring until chocolate melts and mixture is smooth. Stir in sour cream, Grand Marnier, and orange rind. Pour into a greased 13- x 9- x 2-inch pan. Cover and chill at least 8 hours.

Divide mixture into 3 equal portions. Work with 1 portion of mixture at a time, storing remainder in refrigerator. Working quickly, drop chocolate mixture by heaping tablespoonfuls onto wax paper-lined cookie sheets; freeze 10 minutes.

Working with 1 portion at a time, dip pieces into powdered sugar, and roll into 1-inch balls. Return balls to lined cookie sheets, and freeze 1 hour or until firm.

Place sweet baking chocolate in top of a double boiler; bring water to a boil. Reduce heat to low; cook until chocolate melts, stirring often.

Working with 1 portion at a time, place each ball on a candy dipper, or spear each with a wooden pick, and hold over double boiler. Quickly spoon melted chocolate over each ball, allowing excess to drip back into double boiler. Return balls to lined cookie sheets; chill until firm. Place balls in aluminum foil candy cups. Store in an airtight container in refrigerator. Yield: 5½ dozen.

MACADAMIA NUT BRITTLE

1 cup sugar	½ cup chopped macadamia nuts
½ cup light corn syrup	1 tablespoon butter or margarine
¼ cup water	½ teaspoon vanilla extract
¾ cup whole macadamia nuts	⅛ teaspoon baking soda

This golden brittle is a delicious variation of peanut brittle. Find it pictured on page 128.

Combine first 3 ingredients in a large saucepan. Cook over medium heat, stirring constantly, until sugar dissolves. Cover and cook over medium heat 2 to 3 minutes to wash down sugar crystals from sides of pan. Add whole and chopped macadamia nuts; cook until mixture reaches hard crack stage or until a candy thermometer registers 300°, stirring occasionally. Remove from heat. Stir in butter, vanilla, and soda. Working rapidly, pour mixture into a buttered 15- x 10- x 1-inch jellyroll pan, spreading thinly. Cool completely. Break into pieces. Store in an airtight container. Yield: 1 pound.

ORANGE PECANS

1 cup sugar	2¼ cups pecan halves, toasted
⅓ cup orange juice	½ teaspoon grated orange rind
1 teaspoon cream of tartar	

Combine first 3 ingredients in a large heavy saucepan. Cook over low heat, stirring constantly, until sugar dissolves and mixture comes to a boil. Cover and cook 2 to 3 minutes to wash down sugar crystals from sides of pan. Uncover and cook, without stirring, until mixture reaches soft ball stage or until a candy thermometer registers 236°. Remove from heat; beat with a wooden spoon just until mixture begins to thicken. Stir in pecans and orange rind. Working rapidly, drop by rounded teaspoonfuls onto wax paper. Cool. Yield: 2 dozen.

RUSSIAN TEA

Russian Tea
(page 141)

Toasted Pecan Sauce
(page 145)

Gifts from the Kitchen

Christmas Nut Loaf
(page 140)

Christmas Nut Loaf

MARINATED MOZZARELLA

Tie some raffia to a jar of this inspired mozzarella, and you've got a delicious and beautiful gift for any cheese lover.

1 pound mozzarella cheese, cut into
  1-inch cubes
1 (7-ounce) jar roasted red peppers,
  drained and cut into thin strips
2 cloves garlic, cut in half lengthwise
1¼ cups olive oil

1 tablespoon plus 1 teaspoon dried
  Italian seasoning
1 teaspoon dried crushed red pepper
Fresh rosemary or thyme sprigs
  (optional)

Combine cubed cheese, pepper strips, and garlic in a 1-quart jar, and set cheese mixture aside.

Combine olive oil, Italian seasoning, and crushed red pepper. Pour over cheese mixture. Add fresh rosemary or thyme sprigs, if desired. Cover tightly, and shake vigorously. Chill at least 4 hours. Drain and serve with assorted crackers. Store in refrigerator up to 2 weeks. Yield: 4 cups.

CHRISTMAS NUT LOAVES

This recipe yields 3 loaves—perfect for gift-giving. See it wrapped and ready to give on page 139.

1½ cups all-purpose flour
1 teaspoon baking powder
1 teaspoon salt
1½ cups sugar
2 cups coarsely chopped walnuts
3 (10-ounce) packages pitted dates

1 (1-pound) package Brazil nuts,
  shelled
1 (10-ounce) jar maraschino
  cherries, drained
5 large eggs, lightly beaten
1 teaspoon vanilla extract

Grease three 8½- x 4½- x 3-inch loafpans; line bottoms of pans with wax paper. Grease wax paper; set pans aside.

Combine first 4 ingredients in a large bowl; stir in walnuts and next 3 ingredients. Combine eggs and vanilla; add to flour mixture, stirring just until dry ingredients are moistened (batter will be very thick and chunky).

Spoon batter into prepared pans. Bake at 325° for 1 hour or until a wooden pick inserted in center comes out clean. Cool in pans on wire racks 10 minutes; remove from pans. Let cool completely on wire racks; wrap in airtight packages for gift-giving. Yield: 3 loaves.

SWISS CHEESE-MUSTARD BREAD

Pair this hearty bread with sliced ham for an extra special sandwich.

¾ cup milk
½ cup water
¼ cup vegetable oil
5½ to 6 cups all-purpose flour
2 tablespoons sugar
2 teaspoons salt

2 packages active dry yeast
3 large eggs
2 cups (8 ounces) shredded Swiss
  cheese
2 tablespoons prepared mustard
Melted butter or margarine

Combine first 3 ingredients in a small saucepan; heat until warm (120° to 130°).

Combine 2 cups flour, sugar, salt, and yeast in a large mixing bowl. Gradually add liquid mixture to flour mixture, beating at high speed of an electric mixer. Beat 2 more minutes at medium speed. Add eggs, cheese, and mustard, beating just until blended. Gradually stir in enough remaining flour to make a soft dough.

Turn dough out onto a lightly floured surface, and knead until smooth and elastic (about 10 minutes). Cover and let rest 30 minutes. Punch dough down; turn out onto a lightly floured surface, and knead lightly 4 or 5 times. Divide dough in half. Let dough rest 10 minutes. Shape each portion into a ball; place balls in two well-greased 1½-quart round baking dishes, turning to grease tops.

Cover and let rise in a warm place (85°), free from drafts, 1 hour or until doubled in bulk. Bake at 375° for 35 to 40 minutes or until loaves sound hollow when tapped. (Cover with aluminum foil the last 15 minutes of baking to prevent excessive browning, if necessary.) Remove bread from dishes immediately; brush with melted butter. Cool on wire racks; wrap in airtight packages. Yield: 2 loaves.

PRALINE LIQUEUR

2 cups packed dark brown sugar	4 cups pecan pieces, lightly toasted
1 cup sugar	2 vanilla beans, split lengthwise
2½ cups water	4 cups vodka

Combine first 3 ingredients in a medium saucepan, and cook over medium-high heat until sugars dissolve. Bring to a boil; reduce heat, and simmer 5 minutes. Place pecans and vanilla beans in a 1-gallon jar. Pour hot mixture into jar; let cool. Add vodka; stir well. Cover tightly, and store in a dark place at room temperature at least 2 weeks. Shake jar gently once daily.

Pour mixture through a wire-mesh strainer lined with 2 layers of cheesecloth into a bowl, discarding solids. Pour mixture through a wire-mesh strainer lined with a coffee filter into a bowl. Change filter often. (Mixture will drip slowly.) Pour mixture into jars; cover tightly. Store at room temperature. Yield: 4½ cups.

Use this liqueur in coffee, baked apples, or cakes.

RUSSIAN TEA

2 cups sugar	½ cup instant tea mix
2 cups orange-flavored breakfast beverage crystals	1 tablespoon ground cinnamon
⅔ cup presweetened lemonade mix	1 tablespoon ground cloves

Combine all ingredients. Package in an airtight container. Yield: 4½ cups.

DIRECTIONS TO ACCOMPANY GIFT: To serve, place 2 heaping tablespoons mix in a cup or mug. Add ¾ cup boiling water; stir well.

Pop a bag of this fragrant spiced tea mix in a pretty teacup or mug as a thoughtful holiday gift. See examples on page 138.

CHOCOLATE-MACAROON POUND CAKE

1½ cups butter or margarine,
    softened
3 cups sugar
5 large eggs
2½ cups all-purpose flour
2 teaspoons baking powder

½ teaspoon salt
1 cup cocoa
1½ cups buttermilk
2 cups flaked coconut
2 teaspoons vanilla extract
2 teaspoons powdered sugar

Beat butter at medium speed of an electric mixer about 2 minutes or until creamy. Gradually add 3 cups sugar, beating at medium speed 5 to 7 minutes. Add eggs, one at a time, beating just until yellow disappears.

Combine flour and next 3 ingredients; add to butter mixture alternately with buttermilk, beginning and ending with flour mixture. Mix at low speed just until blended after each addition. Stir in coconut and vanilla. Pour batter into a greased and floured 12-cup Bundt pan.

Bake at 350° for 1 hour and 10 minutes or until a wooden pick inserted in center of cake comes out clean. Cool in pan on a wire rack 10 to 15 minutes; remove from pan, and let cool completely on wire rack. Sprinkle with powdered sugar. Wrap in an airtight package for gift-giving. Yield: one 10-inch cake.

WHITE FRUITCAKE

3 cups all-purpose flour, divided
1 cup diced candied citron
1 cup golden raisins
1 cup chopped dates
1 (8-ounce) package sliced candied
    pineapple, cut into eighths
1 (8-ounce) container red or green
    candied cherries (1½ cups)
1 teaspoon baking powder

½ teaspoon salt
2 teaspoons ground cinnamon
2 teaspoons ground allspice
1 teaspoon ground cloves
1 teaspoon ground nutmeg
1½ cups firmly packed brown sugar
1 cup vegetable oil
4 large eggs
1 cup orange juice

We laced this blushing blond fruitcake with a combination of red and green candied cherries for added color.

Draw a circle on a piece of parchment paper, using the bottom of a 10-inch tube pan as a guide. Cut out circle. Set tube pan insert in center of circle, and draw around inside tube; cut out smaller circle. Replace insert in pan; grease bottom only of pan. Line bottom of pan with paper circle; grease paper. Set pan aside.

Combine 1 cup flour, citron, and next 4 ingredients in a large bowl; set aside.

Combine remaining 2 cups flour, baking powder, and next 5 ingredients in a small bowl. Combine brown sugar, oil, and eggs in a large bowl, stirring until smooth. Add flour mixture to brown sugar mixture alternately with orange juice, beginning and ending with flour mixture; stir well after each addition. Stir in fruit mixture.

Spoon batter into prepared pan. Bake at 275° for 2 hours and 45 minutes or until a wooden pick inserted 1 inch from edge comes out clean. Cool in pan on a wire rack. Remove from pan. Wrap in an airtight package. Yield: one 10-inch cake.

CHOCOLATE CHIP GIFT-TUB COOKIES

1 cup butter or margarine, softened
¾ cup firmly packed brown sugar
½ cup sugar
1 large egg
¼ cup sour cream
1 teaspoon vanilla extract

2 cups all-purpose flour
1 teaspoon baking soda
¾ teaspoon salt
1½ cups (9 ounces) semisweet
    chocolate morsels
1 cup coarsely chopped pecans

This cookie dough in a tub is much better than the commercial brands because you make it yourself. Start saving empty plastic tubs for gifts from your kitchen.

Beat butter in a large mixing bowl at medium speed of an electric mixer. Gradually add sugars; beat until blended. Add egg, sour cream, and vanilla; mix well.

Combine flour, soda, and salt; add to butter mixture, mixing well. Stir in chocolate morsels and pecans. Divide dough into two airtight gift containers. Keep refrigerated. Yield: 2 gifts.

DIRECTIONS TO ACCOMPANY GIFT: Store in refrigerator up to 1 week. To bake, drop by tablespoonfuls onto lightly greased cookie sheets. Bake at 375° for 10 to 12 minutes. Cool on wire racks. Yield: 2 dozen.

Super Chocolate Candy

12 ounces peanut butter morsels
1 (4-ounce) package sweet baking
    chocolate

1½ cups pecan halves
½ cup flaked coconut (optional)

Cook peanut butter morsels and chocolate in a medium-size heavy saucepan over low heat until melted, stirring occasionally. Stir in pecans and coconut, if desired. Drop by rounded teaspoonfuls onto wax paper, and let cool completely. Yield: 1¼ pounds.

Rocky Road Clusters

2 cups (12 ounces) semisweet
    chocolate morsels, melted and cooled

1 cup miniature marshmallows
½ cup slivered almonds, toasted

Combine all ingredients, stirring well. Drop by teaspoonfuls onto wax paper. Chill 15 minutes or until firm. Store in an airtight container in the refrigerator. Yield: 3 dozen.

Dried Bean-Soup Mix

1 pound dried kidney beans
1 pound dried yellow lentils
1 pound green split peas
1 pound dried black beans
1 pound dried black-eyed peas
5 teaspoons salt

5 teaspoons dried basil
5 teaspoons dried rosemary
5 teaspoons dried marjoram
2½ teaspoons black pepper
1¼ teaspoons crushed red pepper
5 bay leaves

To prepare dried-bean mix, combine first 5 ingredients in a large bowl. Divide bean mixture into 5 equal portions (about 2½ cups each). Store in airtight containers in a cool, dry place. **To prepare spice mix,** combine salt and remaining 6 ingredients in a bowl. Divide spice mix into 5 equal portions. Store in a small airtight container in a cool, dry place. Yield: 5 gifts.

DIRECTIONS TO ACCOMPANY GIFT: To prepare soup, sort and wash 1 package dried-bean mix, and place in a large Dutch oven. Cover with water to 2 inches above beans; cover and let stand 8 hours. Drain.
    Combine drained bean mixture, 8 cups water, and 1 smoked ham hock in a large Dutch oven; bring to a boil. Add 1 package spice mix, 1 cup chopped onion, and 1 (14.5-ounce) can no-salt-added diced tomatoes (undrained). Cover, reduce heat, and simmer 2 hours. Uncover and cook 1 hour. Discard bay leaf. Remove ham hock from soup. Remove meat from bone; shred meat with 2 forks. Return meat to soup. Yield: 6 servings.

FABULOUS FUDGE SAUCE

2 cups (12 ounces) semisweet
  chocolate morsels
1 (14-ounce) can sweetened
  condensed milk

1 cup miniature marshmallows
½ cup milk
1 teaspoon vanilla extract

Combine all ingredients in a medium saucepan, and cook over medium-low heat until chocolate morsels and marshmallows melt, stirring occasionally. Serve warm over ice cream. Store in refrigerator up to 1 week. Yield: 3¼ cups.

The title of this thick, rich fudge sauce says it all—except maybe how quick and easy it is to make.

TOASTED PECAN SAUCE

½ cup butter or margarine
1¼ cups firmly packed brown sugar
2 tablespoons light corn syrup

½ cup whipping cream
1 cup chopped pecans, toasted

Melt butter in a saucepan over medium heat; add brown sugar and corn syrup, stirring until smooth. Bring to a boil; reduce heat, and simmer 1 minute, stirring constantly. Stir in whipping cream; bring to a boil, stirring constantly. Remove from heat, and stir in chopped pecans. Serve warm over ice cream. Store in refrigerator up to 1 week. Yield: 2¼ cups.

Toasting the pecans will bring out their nutty flavor and help keep them crunchy. See this buttery sauce on page 138.

MARY'S CHILI SAUCE

14 medium-size ripe tomatoes,
   peeled and chopped
2 cups sugar
3 cups finely chopped onion
1 cup chopped green pepper
1 cup chopped sweet red pepper

2 tablespoons salt
3 (3-inch) sticks cinnamon
1 tablespoon whole cloves
1 tablespoon mustard seeds
1 teaspoon ground red pepper
2 cups white vinegar (5% acidity)

Combine first 6 ingredients in a large Dutch oven; bring to a boil. Reduce heat to low, and cook, stirring constantly, until sugar dissolves. Cook, uncovered, 2 more hours or until mixture is thickened, stirring occasionally.

Place cinnamon sticks, cloves, and mustard seeds on a piece of cheesecloth; tie ends of cheesecloth securely with string. Add cheesecloth bag and ground red pepper to tomato mixture; stir in vinegar. Bring to a boil; reduce heat, and simmer, uncovered, 3 to 4 hours or until very thick, stirring occasionally.

Pour hot chili sauce mixture into hot jars, filling to ½ inch from top. Remove air bubbles, and wipe jar rims. Cover at once with metal lids, and screw on bands. Process in boiling water bath 15 minutes. Store in a cool, dry place. Yield: 5 half-pints.

CHRISTMAS SCENT

This spice blend sweetens the air but isn't intended to be eaten.

¼ cup whole cloves
3 (3-inch) sticks cinnamon

3 bay leaves

Combine cloves, cinnamon, and bay leaves in a cheesecloth bag, and tie with raffia or string. Seal in a plastic bag to preserve aroma of spices for gift-giving. Yield: 1 gift.

DIRECTIONS TO ACCOMPANY GIFT: Cut 1 lemon and 1 orange into quarters, and place in a large saucepan. Add 1 quart water and cheesecloth bag of spices; bring to a boil. Reduce heat, and simmer, uncovered, as long as desired, adding water as needed. You can store mixture in the refrigerator for several days and reuse it by replacing the water that boils away.

CRANBERRY-CHERRY RELISH

1 (16-ounce) can whole-berry
  cranberry sauce
1 cup fresh or frozen pitted dark
  cherries
½ cup raisins

¼ cup minced onion
¼ cup firmly packed brown sugar
2 tablespoons balsamic vinegar
1 tablespoon minced fresh ginger

Combine all ingredients in a heavy nonaluminum saucepan. Bring to a boil; reduce heat, and simmer, uncovered, 20 minutes or until thickened. Store in refrigerator. Yield: 2½ cups.

GOLDEN APRICOT JAM

2½ cups water
8 ounces dried apricot halves
2 tablespoons finely grated carrot

2½ teaspoons grated lemon rind
3⅓ cups sugar
3 tablespoons fresh lemon juice

Combine first 4 ingredients in a saucepan; bring to a boil. Cover, reduce heat, and simmer 25 minutes, stirring occasionally. Add sugar and juice; return to a boil, stirring constantly. Reduce heat to low; cook, stirring constantly, 25 minutes or until thickened. Pour hot jam into hot sterilized jars, filling to ¼ inch from top. Remove air bubbles, and wipe jar rims. Cover at once with metal lids, and screw on bands. Process in boiling water bath 5 minutes. Yield: 4 half-pints.

PINK GRAPEFRUIT JELLY

1 (1¾-ounce) package powdered
    pectin

4 cups pink grapefruit juice
5 cups sugar

    Combine pectin and juice in a Dutch oven. Bring to a boil over high heat, stirring constantly. Stir in sugar; return to a boil. Boil 1 minute, stirring constantly. Remove from heat; skim off foam.

    Pour hot grapefruit jelly into hot sterilized jars, filling to ¼ inch from top. Remove air bubbles, and wipe jar rims. Cover at once with metal lids, and screw on bands. Process in boiling water bath 5 minutes. Yield: 8 half-pints.

Only three ingredients, but lots of flavor! Spread this tangy jelly on toast or English muffins.

Glittering Christmas Balls
(page 155)

Easy Peanut Butter Cookies
(page 153)

Children's Workshop

Gingerbread Animal Cookies
(page 153)

PEPPERMINT MILKSHAKES

2 cups milk
½ cup crushed hard peppermint
   candies

4 cups vanilla ice cream

Combine 1 cup milk and ¼ cup crushed candies in container of an electric blender; process 5 seconds. Add 2 cups ice cream; process until smooth, stopping once to scrape down sides. Repeat procedure. Yield: 6 cups.

YOGURT SMOOTHIE

Reward your young helpers with this smoothie that's both healthy and delicious.

1 ripe banana, peeled and cut into
   pieces
1 (8-ounce) carton vanilla low-fat
   yogurt

1 cup orange juice
2 tablespoons sugar

Combine all ingredients in container of an electric blender. Process 2 minutes or until smooth, stopping once to scrape down sides. Yield: 2½ cups.

CRUNCHY SNACK MIX

4 cups bite-size pretzels
3 cups honey graham cereal
2 cups crispy wheat cereal squares
1½ cups pecan halves

¾ cup butter or margarine, melted
1½ tablespoons Worcestershire sauce
2 tablespoons light brown sugar

Combine first 4 ingredients in a 15- x 10- x 1-inch jellyroll pan.
Combine butter, Worcestershire sauce, and brown sugar; pour over cereal mixture, stirring to coat. Bake at 250° for 1 hour, stirring every 15 minutes. Remove from oven, and cool. Store in an airtight container. Yield: 8 cups.

GABRIEL'S HORNS

¼ cup creamy peanut butter
2 cups original flavor corn snacks (we
   tested with original flavor Bugles)

3 (2-ounce) squares chocolate candy
   coating, melted

Spoon creamy peanut butter into a small plastic bag; snip a small hole in corner of bag. Squeeze a small amount of peanut butter into each corn snack.
Dip peanut butter-filled corn snacks into melted candy coating, and place on wax paper to dry. Store in an airtight container. Yield: 3½ dozen.

CARAMEL-CHOCOLATE STICKY BUNS

1 (15-ounce) container ready-to-
   spread coconut-pecan frosting
1 cup pecan halves

2 (10- to 12-ounce) cans refrigerated
   buttermilk biscuits
20 milk chocolate kisses

Spread coconut-pecan frosting in a lightly greased 9-inch square pan. Top with pecan halves.

Separate biscuits; flatten to about ¼-inch thickness. Place a chocolate kiss on each biscuit. Fold biscuits in half; press edges to seal. Arrange over pecans, flat sides down. Bake at 375° for 28 to 30 minutes or until lightly browned. Cool in pan on a wire rack 5 minutes; invert onto a serving plate, and serve immediately. Yield: 10 servings.

ZEBRAS

1 (8-ounce) container frozen
   whipped topping, thawed

1 (9-ounce) package chocolate
   wafers

Spoon 1 tablespoon whipped topping on top of 12 wafers; place on a jellyroll pan. Top each with a second wafer and an additional tablespoon whipped topping. Complete each stack with a third wafer. Gently spread top and sides of wafer stacks with remaining whipped topping. Cover and chill overnight. Yield: 12 servings.

SNOWBALL SANDWICH COOKIES

6 ounces white chocolate,
   chopped

2 (12-ounce) boxes Danish wedding
   cookies

Little fingers will enjoy dipping these cookies in melted chocolate.

Melt white chocolate in a heavy saucepan over low heat, stirring occasionally. Dip flat sides of half the cookies in white chocolate, and top with flat sides of remaining cookies. Let stand until white chocolate is firm. Yield: 4 dozen.

UNBELIEVABLES

1 (16-ounce) jar crunchy peanut
   butter

2 small eggs
1½ cups sugar

Combine all ingredients in a medium mixing bowl; beat at medium speed of an electric mixer until blended. Drop by rounded teaspoonfuls onto ungreased cookie sheets. Flatten cookies in a crisscross pattern with a fork. Bake at 375° for 8 to 10 minutes or until edges are golden. Cool 5 minutes on cookies sheets; remove cookies to wire racks, and let cool completely. Yield: 3 dozen.

Ornaments You Can Eat

These candylike cookie ornaments are safe to eat, and the dough is pliable enough for small hands to shape.

¼ cup butter or margarine, softened
⅓ cup light corn syrup
1 teaspoon vanilla extract
1 (16-ounce) package powdered
   sugar, sifted and divided

Green paste food coloring
Red cinnamon candies
Powdered sugar
Tubes of decorator frosting
Assorted sprinkles

Combine first 3 ingredients in a large mixing bowl; beat at medium speed of an electric mixer until blended. Gradually add half of powdered sugar, beating until smooth. Stir in enough remaining powdered sugar to make a stiff dough, kneading with hands, if necessary.

Divide dough in half; wrap 1 portion in plastic wrap, and set aside. Knead green food coloring into remaining portion of dough.

To make wreaths, shape green dough into 18 (1-inch) balls. Roll each ball into a 5-inch rope, and connect ends of rope to form a circle. Decorate circles with red cinnamon candies to resemble wreaths.

To make cutout ornaments, roll out remaining portion of dough to about ¼-inch thickness on a surface lightly dusted with powdered sugar. Cut into desired shapes, using 2-inch cookie cutters. Punch a hole in the top of each ornament, using a stir stick straw. Decorate ornaments with frosting and assorted sprinkles.

Lay wreaths and ornaments flat on wax paper; set aside to partially dry (about 4 hours). Remove from wax paper; transfer to wire racks. Let dry 24 hours.

To hang, tie ornaments with ribbon. Yield: 3 dozen.

GINGERBREAD ANIMAL COOKIES

½ cup shortening
½ cup sugar
½ cup molasses
¼ cup water
3 cups all-purpose flour
½ teaspoon baking soda
¾ teaspoon salt
¾ teaspoon ground ginger
¼ teaspoon ground nutmeg
Tubes of decorator frosting (optional)
Assorted sprinkles (optional)

Beat shortening at medium speed of an electric mixer until fluffy; gradually add sugar, beating well. Add molasses and water; beat well.

Combine flour and next 4 ingredients; add to shortening mixture, mixing well. Cover and chill dough several hours.

Work with one-fourth of dough at a time; store remainder in refrigerator. Roll dough to ¼-inch thickness on an ungreased cookie sheet. Cut with assorted 2- to 3-inch animal-shaped cookie cutters; remove excess dough. Bake at 375° for 6 to 8 minutes. Cool 2 minutes. Remove to wire racks to cool. Repeat procedure with remaining dough. Decorate with frosting and sprinkles, if desired. Yield: about 4 dozen.

Let your kids' creativity run wild with these fun gingerbread cookies. The photo on pages 148 and 149 shows decorating suggestions.

CHOCOLATE CHIP SQUARES

2 (20-ounce) packages refrigerated sliceable chocolate chip cookie dough
2 (8-ounce) packages cream cheese, softened
1½ cups sugar
2 large eggs

Freeze rolls of cookie dough; slice 1 roll of frozen cookie dough into 40 (⅛-inch-thick) slices. Arrange cookie slices in a well-greased 15- x 10- x 1-inch jellyroll pan. Press cookie dough together to form bottom crust. Set aside.

Beat cream cheese at high speed of an electric mixer until fluffy; gradually add sugar, and mix well. Add eggs, one at a time, beating after each addition. Pour cream cheese mixture over cookie dough layer in pan.

Slice remaining cookie dough into 40 (⅛-inch-thick) slices; arrange over cream cheese mixture. Bake at 350° for 45 minutes. Cool and cut into squares. Yield: 4 dozen.

EASY PEANUT BUTTER COOKIES

1 large egg, lightly beaten
1 cup chunky peanut butter
1 cup sugar
36 milk chocolate kisses, unwrapped

Combine first 3 ingredients; shape into ¾-inch balls. Place on ungreased cookie sheets. Bake at 350° for 10 minutes. Immediately press a chocolate kiss in center of each cookie; remove to wire racks to cool. Yield: 3 dozen.

This is a great recipe for children to help make. Find the cookies on page 148.

SNOWBALL SURPRISES

1 cup butter or margarine, softened
½ cup sugar
1 teaspoon vanilla extract
2 cups all-purpose flour

1 cup finely chopped pecans
10 chocolate-coated peppermint
    patties (we tested with York)
Sifted powdered sugar

Beat butter at medium speed of an electric mixer until creamy; gradually add sugar, beating until light and fluffy. Stir in vanilla.

Stir in flour and pecans, mixing well; cover and chill at least 1 hour.

Cut peppermint patties into fourths. Press 1 tablespoon dough around each candy piece, forming a ball. Place on ungreased cookie sheets.

Bake at 350° for 12 minutes. (Cookies will not brown.) Cool 5 minutes on cookie sheets, and roll in powdered sugar. Place on wire racks to cool. Yield: 40 cookies.

PRALINE GRAHAMS

1 (5⅓-ounce) package graham
    crackers
¾ cup butter or margarine

½ cup sugar
1 cup chopped pecans

Separate each graham cracker into four sections. Arrange crackers in an ungreased 15- x 10- x 1-inch jellyroll pan with edges touching.

Melt butter in a saucepan; stir in sugar and pecans. Bring to a boil; cook 3 minutes, stirring often. Spread mixture evenly over graham crackers.

Bake at 300° for 12 minutes. Remove from pan, and cool on wax paper. Yield: 3½ dozen.

SINFUL SEVEN-LAYER COOKIES

Kids of all ages can participate in this cookie preparation. Allow them to layer all the yummy ingredients.

½ cup butter or margarine
1 cup graham cracker crumbs
1 cup (6 ounces) semisweet chocolate
    morsels
1 cup (6 ounces) butterscotch
    morsels

1 cup flaked coconut
1 (14-ounce) can sweetened
    condensed milk
1 cup chopped pecans

Place butter in a 13- x 9- x 2-inch baking dish. Preheat dish in oven at 350° for 5 minutes or until butter melts. Layer graham cracker crumbs and next 3 ingredients over butter. Pour condensed milk over coconut; top with pecans. Bake at 350° for 30 minutes. Cool on a wire rack; cut into squares. Yield: 15 cookies.

CARAMELTS

1 (14-ounce) package caramels
¼ cup milk

4 cups crisp rice cereal
1 cup salted roasted peanuts

Unwrap caramels, and place in a large saucepan. Add milk; cook over low heat until caramels melt, stirring often. Remove from heat, and stir in cereal and peanuts.

Spoon into a buttered 8-inch square pan. Firmly press mixture into pan. Cool completely in pan on a wire rack. Cut into squares. Yield: 16 squares.

GLITTERING CHRISTMAS BALLS

2½ cups graham cracker crumbs
1 cup sifted powdered sugar
½ cup finely chopped pecans
½ cup miniature candy-coated chocolate pieces
1 cup flaked coconut (optional)

1 cup chocolate syrup
1½ teaspoons vanilla extract
10 (2-ounce) squares vanilla-flavored candy coating
Assorted sprinkles and colored sugar

Children will enjoy decorating these glittering balls with colorful varieties of candy sprinkles and colored sugar. They're pictured on page 148.

Combine first 4 ingredients in a large bowl; add coconut, if desired. Stir in syrup and vanilla. Shape into 1-inch balls, and chill 1 hour.

Place candy coating in top of a double boiler; bring water to a boil. Reduce heat to low; cook until coating melts. Remove from heat.

Dip each ball into candy coating; place on wax paper, and let dry. Decorate with candy sprinkles and colored sugar. Yield: 5 dozen.

PEPPERMINT CANDY CUPS

12 ounces vanilla-flavored candy coating
¾ cup crushed hard peppermint candy

Petits fours paper cups

Create this minty confection in a twinkling. A child can crush the mints while an adult melts the candy coating.

Place candy coating in a 2-quart glass bowl; microwave at MEDIUM (50% power) 3 to 4 minutes or until melted, stirring after 2 minutes. Stir in candy.

Spoon mixture evenly into petits fours paper cups, filling ¾ full. Chill until firm. Store in an airtight container. Yield: 3 dozen.

Index

Metric Equivalents

The recipes that appear in this cookbook use the standard United States method for measuring liquid and dry or solid ingredients (teaspoons, tablespoons, and cups). The information on this chart is provided to help cooks outside the U.S. successfully use these recipes. All equivalents are approximate.

METRIC EQUIVALENTS FOR DIFFERENT TYPES OF INGREDIENTS

A standard cup measure of a dry or solid ingredient will vary in weight depending on the type of ingredient. A standard cup of liquid is the same volume for any type of liquid. Use the following chart when converting standard cup measures to grams (weight) or milliliters (volume).

Standard Cup	Fine Powder (ex. flour)	Grain (ex. rice)	Granular (ex. sugar)	Liquid Solids (ex. butter)	Liquid (ex. milk)
1	140 g	150 g	190 g	200 g	240 ml
¾	105 g	113 g	143 g	150 g	180 ml
⅔	93 g	100 g	125 g	133 g	160 ml
½	70 g	75 g	95 g	100 g	120 ml
⅓	47 g	50 g	63 g	67 g	80 ml
¼	35 g	38 g	48 g	50 g	60 ml
⅛	18 g	19 g	24 g	25 g	30 ml

USEFUL EQUIVALENTS FOR DRY INGREDIENTS BY WEIGHT

(To convert ounces to grams, multiply the number of ounces by 30.)

1 oz	=	¹⁄₁₆ lb	=	30 g
4 oz	=	¼ lb	=	120 g
8 oz	=	½ lb	=	240 g
12 oz	=	¾ lb	=	360 g
16 oz	=	1 lb	=	480 g

USEFUL EQUIVALENTS FOR LENGTH

(To convert inches to centimeters, multiply the number of inches by 2.5.)

1 in				=	2.5 cm	
6 in	=	½ ft		=	15 cm	
12 in	=	1 ft		=	30 cm	
36 in	=	3 ft	= 1 yd	=	90 cm	
40 in				=	100 cm	= 1 m

USEFUL EQUIVALENTS FOR LIQUID INGREDIENTS BY VOLUME

¼ tsp						=	1 ml	
½ tsp						=	2 ml	
1 tsp						=	5 ml	
3 tsp	=	1 tbls		=	½ fl oz	=	15 ml	
		2 tbls	= ⅛ cup	=	1 fl oz	=	30 ml	
		4 tbls	= ¼ cup	=	2 fl oz	=	60 ml	
		5⅓ tbls	= ⅓ cup	=	3 fl oz	=	80 ml	
		8 tbls	= ½ cup	=	4 fl oz	=	120 ml	
		10⅔ tbls	= ⅔ cup	=	5 fl oz	=	160 ml	
		12 tbls	= ¾ cup	=	6 fl oz	=	180 ml	
		16 tbls	= 1 cup	=	8 fl oz	=	240 ml	
		1 pt	= 2 cups	=	16 fl oz	=	480 ml	
		1 qt	= 4 cups	=	32 fl oz	=	960 ml	
					33 fl oz	=	1000 ml	= 1 l

USEFUL EQUIVALENTS FOR COOKING/OVEN TEMPERATURES

	Fahrenheit	Celsius	Gas Mark
Freeze Water	32° F	0° C	
Room Temperature	68° F	20° C	
Boil Water	212° F	100° C	
Bake	325° F	160° C	3
	350° F	180° C	4
	375° F	190° C	5
	400° F	200° C	6
	425° F	220° C	7
	450° F	230° C	8
Broil			Grill